Studies and documents on cultural policies

Recent titles in this series:

For a complete list of titles see page 73

Cultural policy in the
Ukrainian Soviet Socialist Republic

G. Shevchuk

unesco

Published in 1982 by the United Nations Educational,
Scientific and Cultural Organization,
7 place de Fontenoy, 75700 Paris
Printed by Imprimerie des Presses Universitaires
de France, Vendôme

ISBN 92-3-101969-4
French edition: 92-3-201969-8

Preface

The purpose of this series is to show how cultural policies are planned and implemented in various Member States.

As cultures differ, so does the approach to them; it is for each Member State to determine its cultural policy and methods according to its own conception of culture, its socio-economic system, political ideology and technical development. However, the methods of cultural policy (like those of general development policy) have certain common problems; these are largely institutional, administrative and financial in nature, and the need has increasingly been stressed for exchanging experiences and information about them. This series, each issue of which follows as far as possible a similar pattern so as to make comparison easier, is mainly concerned with these technical aspects of cultural policy.

In general, the studies deal with the principles and methods of cultural policy, the evaluation of cultural needs, administrative structures and management, planning and financing, the organization of resources, legislation, budgeting, public and private institutions, cultural content in education, cultural autonomy and decentralization, the training of personnel, institutional infrastructures for meeting specific cultural needs, the safeguarding of the cultural heritage, institutions for the dissemination of the arts, international cultural co-operation and other related subjects.

The studies, which cover countries belonging to differing social and economic systems, geographical areas and levels of development, present, therefore, a wide variety of approaches and methods in cultural policy. Taken as a whole, they can provide guidelines to countries which have yet to establish cultural policies, while all countries, especially those seeking new formulations of such policies, can profit by the experience already gained.

This study was prepared for Unesco by Professor G. Shevchuk of the Cultural Institute of Kiev.

The opinions expressed are the author's and do not necessarily reflect the view of Unesco.

Contents

Contents

Introduction

The Ukrainian Soviet Socialist Republic is a socialist state expressing the aspirations and interests of the workers, peasants and intellectuals. Occupying an area of 603,700 square kilometres, the country has a population of 50 million. Its capital is the hero city of Kiev, with a population of 2,200,000.

The Ukrainian SSR emerged as a sovereign national state as a result of the victory of the Great October Socialist Revolution in 1917, which was achieved through the efforts of the workers and the poorest peasants under the direction of the Communist Party, organized and led by Vladimir Il'ich Lenin. On 25 December 1917 the First All-Ukrainian Congress of Soviets proclaimed the establishment of the Ukraine as a Republic of Soviets.

The Ukrainian Soviet Socialist Republic was one of the early advocates of the idea that the Soviet republics should unite to form a single unified state, since this would provide the most favourable conditions for the building of socialism and the defence of its achievements. In 1922 the Soviet peoples freely and voluntarily decided, on the basis of full equality, to join together into a single state, the Union of Soviet Socialist Republics, which is made up of fifteen Union Republics.

Through their constructive efforts, the Soviet people, an integral part of which is the people of the Ukrainian SSR, have built an advanced socialist society, in which the revolution in science and technology is combined with the advantages of the socialist economic system, intensive economic development methods are applied, so that unprecedented levels of production are attained, and the whole system of social relationships operates satisfactorily. Soviet culture is highly developed; it is socialist in content, nationalist and diverse in form and internationalist in spirit and character.

Another distinctive feature of socialist reality is the Soviet way of life, which provides every active individual with the opportunity to develop

9

his intellectual and physical capacities to the full. The result is that the interests and needs of the individual are in harmony with those of society. This harmonious relationship is the foundation of true freedom under socialism and communism.

The Soviet people are putting all their innovative ability into the historic and universally important task of building a communist society; cultural policy is part and parcel of that effort.

The purpose of this study is to throw light on the nature and aims of the Ukrainian Soviet state's cultural policy, through which the culture of the Ukrainian people has taken shape, developed and reached its present high standard.

The nature and conduct
of cultural policy

The cultural policy of the Ukrainian Soviet Socialist Republic is designed to ensure that all workers have access to the cultural wealth created by mankind. It is aimed at the all-round development of the personality, so that everyone possesses the qualities required of an active builder of a new life—spiritual strength, moral purity and physical fitness.

In shaping its cultural policy, the Soviet state is guided by the principle that the political, economic and spiritual spheres of life are interrelated and exercise a mutual influence on each other, though economic factors are the predominant influence on the whole social process.

As a result of the socialist revolution, all that was best in the realm of culture, science and art passed into the hands of the workers. Schools, libraries, museums, theatres, cinemas, the radio, the press, literature and art became the means whereby all this was made available to the masses. Culture became an important factor in all socialist reforms, and cultural development, an organic element in the functioning of Soviet society. The profound economic, political and ideological changes in the life of society that resulted from the victory of the socialist revolution created the necessary objective and subjective conditions for the successful application of a cultural policy. This policy was embodied in the plan for a cultural revolution worked out by Lenin, who elaborated the theory behind it; and it became an integral part of the overall plan for the building of socialism in our country.

The main objective of Lenin's plan for a cultural revolution was the creation of a new socialist culture that would be a powerful weapon in the hands of the workers in their efforts to build a socialist society free from the exploitation of man by man.

As the cultural policy is put into practice, the cultural level of the masses rises, and they become more active in the organization of the new regime, in the government, in the management of the economy and in work to provide the materials and equipment required for the building of

11

socialism. A cultural policy is one of the principal prerequisites for the building of socialism. Its basic principles are the use of the historical method in formulating the aims of cultural development; the recognition of the class character of culture; the affirmation of the lofty ideals of the struggle for social justice; the continuity of cultural development; humanism; the unity of cultural content and form; the unity of the national and international constituents of culture; and universal access to cultural values. These principles underwent further development and refinement in accordance with historical conditions and the nature and content of the objectives that were to be attained. Cultural policy is focused primarily on the integrated ideological and political education of Soviet citizens, and its application to labour and morality, and on encouraging their intellectual progress.

The cultural policy embraces all aspects of the intellectual life of socialist society; together they form a complete system covering all aspects of that society—its political, ideological, moral and aesthetic aspects, the organization of public education, the development of a new work ethic and the promotion of the artistic and technical creativity of the people. The cultural policy is executed in such a way as to encourage the harmonious development, in all their richness and diversity, of all the constituent functions of culture—cognition, the transformation of society, symbolism, evaluation and communication.

The cultural policy is based on the norms and principles of Lenin regarding the introduction and development of socialist culture and its gradual transformation into communist culture and on the methods he advocated. Socialist culture as a whole, as well as its constituent parts—education, science, literature and art—is steeped in Marxist-Leninist ideology; it has a class character, and reflects the interests of all the workers; its purpose is a noble one—to contribute to the spiritual development of society.

Soviet cultural policy expresses the interests of all the people and is ardently supported by them. As Lenin wrote,

The workers aspire to knowledge because they must have it if they are to be victorious. Nine-tenths of the working masses have realized that knowledge is a weapon in their struggle for liberation, that their failures were due to a lack of education and that it is now up to them to make education really accessible to all. . . . They see how essential education is if they are to win the war they are waging.

The state's cultural policy is laid down in the new constitution, the Basic Law of the Ukrainian Soviet Socialist Republic, which was adopted in 1977 and takes into account the historical, national and other characteristics of the republic. The constitution reflects the outstanding achievements that have been made in the implementation of the cultural policy—the high level of science and culture and the strong moral fibre and ideological

12

consciousness of the people. It also sets targets for a high level of cultural development in the future and makes it incumbent on the state to provide economic, political and ideological conditions that are conducive to the application and implementation of the cultural policy, in accordance with the humanistic character of the socialist state.

The state carries out its activities through the Soviets of People's Deputies and their subordinate bodies, which are responsible for administering all branches of state, economic and socio-cultural institutions.

The cultural policy is carried out scientifically, on the basis of cultural development plans drawn up at the local and national levels and financial support for cultural activities.

There are several types of plans: a short-term, annual plan, a medium-term plan covering five, ten or fifteen years, and a long-term plan for a period of twenty or thirty years. The plans are based on estimates of population growth, economic needs and forecasts of scientific and technological progress. Planning is global in character; it has a 'vertical' dimension (by branch of culture) and a 'horizontal' (or territorial) dimension.

The plans provide for every branch of culture and science to be developed in conjunction with the needs of the national economy and the need to satisfy as fully as possible the spiritual requirements of the people.

Scientific development is ensured by applying the principle of strictly co-ordinated and synchronized planning and that of the interaction of science, technology and production. The latest methods, including mathematical models, are widely used in planning. The purpose of planning is to ensure that every component of culture and the system as a whole develop as far as possible in accordance with the objective laws of the development of society and to minimize the uncontrolled development of spiritual culture; in other words, to ensure that the development of the spiritual life of society is in line with the precepts of the objective laws of socialism.

Appropriate financing is provided for the attainment of the targets laid down in the plans. It comes from three sources: funds from the state budget, funds drawn from the net profits of state and co-operative enterprises, and special funds derived from receipts at theatrical performances, concerts, film shows and other kinds of paid entertainment.

This type of system, embracing management, planning and finance, ensures the harmonious development of all that goes to make up culture. Under the constitution, public organizations such as trade unions, the Young Communist League (Komsomol), co-operatives and other mass associations of workers have a great deal of responsibility for carrying out cultural policy. Through such organizations large numbers of workers take an active part in the management of state affairs and in decisions concerning political, economic and socio-cultural matters. In accordance with the constitution, the Communist Party of the Soviet Union, which is dedicated to the people and serves its interests, is the leader and guide of

Soviet society and the centre of its political system and of state and public organizations.

The constitution assigns an important role in the nation's life and, accordingly, in the execution of cultural policy, to workers' collectives in industrial and agricultural enterprises and associations and in educational and scientific institutions. They take part in discussions and decisions concerning state and public affairs, in the planning of production and of social development, in the training and placement of personnel, in discussions and decisions concerning the management of enterprises and institutions, the improvement of working and living conditions and the use of resources earmarked for production and for socio-cultural activities. The participation of workers' collectives in implementing cultural policy is especially beneficial because it provides workers with a practical opportunity to make use of their intellectual faculties and develop new ones.

The constitution gives official recognition to the human relations between the state and the individual that resulted from the socialist transformation of society. It provides the necessary conditions for the free and harmonious development of the personality. In accordance with the principle that 'the free development of each person is the prerequisite for the free development of all', the state seeks to give citizens even more opportunities than they already have to use their creative energies and aptitudes and develop them in every possible way.

The state guarantees the equality of all citizens before the law in economic, political and cultural life, irrespective of origin, social status, property, race and nationality, sex, education, language, religious attitude, nature and type of occupation, place of residence and other circumstances. Women enjoy equal rights with men.

The state gives its citizens basic rights and defines their duties. Some are direct rights: the right to education, to have an occupation and to engage in scientific and artistic activity; others concern the creation of conditions for the exercise of the direct rights. Among these are the right to work, rest, health care, housing, security in old age or sickness and in the case of full or partial disability or the loss of the bread-winner. The right of freedom of conscience is also guaranteed, that is, the right to profess or not to profess a religion, the right to celebrate religious rites or carry on anti-religious propaganda. Incitement to religious hostility and hatred is forbidden.

A great deal is done to ensure that everyone enjoys the right to education. Education at all levels is free; secondary education is compulsory for all young people; there is an extensive and well-developed system of vocational and technical, specialized secondary and higher education, which is adapted to the needs of life and production; correspondence and evening courses are provided; pupils and students can obtain state grants and benefits; there is no charge for textbooks; the language of instruction

14

is the pupil's own language; and pupils have every opportunity for independent study.

The right of citizens to enjoy the benefits of culture is ensured by arrangements giving them free access to the treasures of national and world culture that are found in state and public collections; by the development of cultural and educational institutions and their even distribution throughout the country; by the development of television and radio, the publishing of books and periodicals and the provision of public libraries; and by the expansion of cultural exchange with other countries.

Citizens are free to engage in artistic, scientific and technical activities, and every encouragement is given to scientific research, the development of inventions and rationalizing techniques, and work in literature and the arts. The state provides the necessary material conditions for such activities; it supports the work of voluntary scientists' and artists' societies and introduces inventions and rationalizing techniques into the economy and other spheres of national life. It protects the copyrights and patents of inventors and rationalizers.

The cultural policy is being successfully carried out, thanks to the growth of the country's socialist economy, the ownership of which is vested in the people. In the early 1930s, unemployment was wiped out in the Ukraine SSR for all time. The economy progresses steadily, without interruption, with the result that there is full employment, living standards are constantly rising, and everything necessary is done to satisfy the spiritual needs of the people.

Economic development has led to the success of the social programme, and the material and spiritual needs of the population have been more fully satisfied. In 1980, for example, four-fifths of the national income was spent on their welfare—on housing and the construction of buildings for socio-cultural purposes. Moreover, the funds allocated to socio-cultural activities from the profits of state, co-operative, trade union and other public enterprises and associations have increased from year to year. In 1965, they amounted to 6.9 thousand million roubles and in 1978 they reached the figure of 16.5 thousand million.

The salaries of workers and employees in the republic are 1.4 times as much as they were ten years ago, and the wages of collective farmers 1.6 times as much. In recent years a great deal has been done to increase the remuneration of workers and employees, and 14 million wage-earners have received increases.

Apart from wages, workers receive substantial sums from social consumption funds, and these benefits increase every year. They include such things as free medical service, care of mothers and new-born babies, free education at all levels of the educational system, further job training, student grants, paid annual holidays, free or cut-rate accommodation in sanatoriums and rest-homes, an allowance for children in pre-school institutions, old-age pensions and disability benefits and a number of other

15

benefits and advantages. The state expends 200 roubles for every new-born baby (care in maternity hospital, free home assistance by trained workers for new mothers). At the birth of a third child, the family receives a lump sum grant from the state, and at the birth of a fourth child, a monthly allowance in addition to the lump sum allocation.

The annual cost of maintaining a child in a nursery is 500 roubles and in a kindergarten 450 roubles. The state defrays four-fifths of the cost, the parents covering the rest. The state expends 160 roubles a year on each child in a general education establishment, and over 200 roubles in the case of a child in a school that keeps open late to enable working parents to collect children after normal school hours—an increasingly common practice; it spends 640 roubles a year on each student in a technical school and over 1,000 roubles for each university student.

More and more general service facilities are being made available to the population which means that much less time has to be devoted to domestic chores at the end of the working day. Since the establishment of the Soviet regime, the working week for workmen and office workers has been reduced by 18 hours; it is now 41 hours. Workers have two days off per week, and this makes it possible for them to devote more time to the upbringing of their children, make better use of their free time and improve their cultural and educational standard.

Such, then, is the nature of the cultural policy, the principles that govern it, the constitutional framework that underlies it and the economic and political conditions in which it is carried out.

Implementation
of cultural policy
during the period
of socialist construction

When the Soviet regime was established, the Ukrainian people, who had endured centuries of national and social oppression under the tsars, embarked on the building of a national culture in their own sovereign state. Special bodies were set up in the republic with responsibility for carrying out the cultural policy of the state. They were faced with the enormously complicated task of evolving a new culture and reorganizing the entire spiritual life of the nation.

Before the Soviet regime came to power, 76 per cent of the people of the Ukraine were illiterate. Most of the schools were primary schools, none of which used Ukrainian as the language of instruction. The few secondary and higher educational establishments that did exist were attended by children of the ruling and exploiting classes. Only 34,600 persons out of the Ukraine's total population of over 35 million had received any vocational training. Women were particularly discriminated against in the matter of civic rights and education. At the beginning of the twentieth century, only 35 women had had a higher education. There were only 3,000 libraries for all the population centres in the Ukraine, which numbered 55,000. It was illegal to publish books and newspapers in Ukrainian.

The great proletarian writer Maxim Gorky remarked bitterly in 1916: 'The situation of the Ukrainian working people today is tragic in the extreme. The tsarist cutthroats give them no chance to develop their language, literature and art. What the tsarist government is doing to the Ukrainians and other oppressed peoples is a crime beyond words.'

After the October victory, the Soviet Government, on the personal initiative of V. I. Lenin, issued a series of decrees aimed at creating the conditions required for the widest participation of the masses in the building up of their culture. Special mention should be made of the Declaration of the Rights of the Peoples of Russia, which abolished all national

17

and religious privileges, established the equality and sovereignty of all peoples and guaranteed their free development.

Abolished, too, were the tsarist restrictions on the rights of workers to have access to the riches of the mind, the division of society into classes and the limitations on the rights of women.

With the establishment of the Soviet regime, the people of the Ukraine, for the first time in their long history, began to use their own language freely in public and political life and in education, science and culture. The Ukrainian language, both spoken and written, became the property of the working masses.

One of the first steps taken by the Soviet regime was to arrange for the protection of historical and cultural monuments and to turn them over to the people, using whatever was most worth while and progressive as a foundation for the building of a new culture. The schools and all the cultural institutions passed into the hands of the state and became public property. Free education was introduced for all, both boys and girls, instruction being given in their mother tongue.

The workers, emancipated by the Soviet regime, were thirsty for knowledge. Schools, clubs, community centres, libraries, people's universities, classes, and choral, musical and theatrical clubs were opened all over the republic. The Ukrainian SSR, like other Soviet republics, became an immense classroom.

In March 1919, the Ukrainian people adopted the first constitution in their long history. It consolidated the great achievements of the workers in their struggle for social and national emancipation and proclaimed the equality of all the workers in the country, irrespective of race and nationality. It established extensive democratic rights for workers: freedom of speech, freedom of the press, freedom of assembly; freedom for the development of the Ukrainian language and Ukrainian culture; the right to education; and it also guaranteed the exercise of these rights.

Under the constitution, power was vested in the people through the Soviets of Workers', Peasants' and Soldiers' Deputies. The Soviets carried out their activities under the direction of the Communist Party in close association with the mass public organizations—trade unions, the Leninist Young Communist League, the Committees of Poor Peasants, co-operatives and other organizations.

After the victory of the Soviet regime, the Communist Party defined its cultural policy, which was embodied in the Second Party Programme, adopted in March 1919. This programme defined the basic aim of cultural policy during the period of transition from capitalism to socialism—the complete reorganization of the country's cultural life.

It was a complex and difficult process, inasmuch as there was no precedent for such a far-reaching reform. To make matters worse, the counter-revolutionary forces of the old regime, with the support of foreign imperialists, involved our country in a long and exhausting war. Famine and

18

epidemics spread throughout the country, hundreds of thousands of waifs and orphans roamed the towns and countryside. It took a great deal of time, energy and resources to set things right.

The Communist Party and Lenin himself were unsparing in their solicitude for the Ukrainian people and helped them to carry out the cultural policy. The document written by Lenin and adopted by the Communist Party at the close of 1919, 'On Soviet power in the Ukraine', was of the greatest importance. The Central Committee of the party ordered that steps be taken to ensure the all-round development of the Ukrainian language and Ukrainian culture. Help was made available to the Ukrainians in the form of financial assistance, school and laboratory equipment, textbooks, books on teaching methods, and other materials.

Among the major factors ensuring the successful implementation of the cultural policy were the arrangements for cultural co-operation among the different republics that were developed on a broad scale soon after the establishment of the Soviet regime. The year 1922 marked the turning-point not only in this sphere but in the entire life of the Ukrainian people, for it saw the voluntary unification of the Soviet republics to form the Union of Soviet Socialist Republics, on the basis of the principle of socialist federalism, that is, the principle of full equality of rights and duties, mutual trust and fraternal co-operation between all the peoples. The development and consolidation of a unified, multinational socialist state opened up still wider prospects for the social, economic and cultural advancement of all the peoples, including the Ukrainian.

Cultural policy, like the whole programme of socialist construction, is carried out according to a systematic plan. There are annual plans for the development of the national economy, and also five-year plans, an integral part of which is the plan for cultural construction.

One of the priorities was the eradication of mass illiteracy and the improvement of the general educational level of the population. A special body was set up for this purpose—the All-Ukrainian Extraordinary Commission to Combat Illiteracy. It directed a nationwide campaign, with the active participation of trade unions, the Komsomol, the Committees of Poor Peasants, the co-operatives and the voluntary association 'Down with Illiteracy', which was formed in 1922. The whole literate population took part in the campaign. Centres and schools for illiterates were organized throughout the country. Hundreds of thousands of people flocked to such centres in the 1920s and millions in the early 1930s.

Besides receiving a general education, students acquired political, technical and agricultural knowledge which enabled them to take an active part in the building of socialism. During the first twenty years of the Soviet regime in the Ukrainian SSR nearly 20 million people learned to read and write.

The whole system of public education and training was radically reorganized. A completely new type of educational system was established,

19

in which school education and out-of-school education were harmoniously combined. The school education system consisted of general education schools, vocational and technical schools for training highly skilled workers for the most common occupations, and secondary and higher education institutions. The out-of-school education system consisted of a network of clubs and museums, young pioneer palaces and centres, libraries, parks of culture and rest, tourist centres, etc.

As the national economy recovered from the effects of a destructive war and embarked on the path of socialism, the economic situation of the Ukrainian SSR improved, and the appropriations for science and education were increased. Whereas expenditure on education and science for the period 1928-32 amounted to 1,610,300 roubles, for the period 1933-37 it reached the figure of 7,602,800 roubles. Seventy-one per cent of republic and local budgets was allocated to socio-cultural needs, and this made it possible to increase the scale of cultural action considerably.

At the same time, much was done to improve the material situation and working conditions of teachers, scientists, writers and artists. Their remuneration was increased as the country's economy grew stronger, and towards the mid-1930s academic degrees (Candidate of Sciences, Doctor of Sciences) and professional grades (junior scientific worker, senior scientific worker, lecturer and professor) were introduced for researchers and teachers; honorary distinctions were also conferred, such as honoured scientist, honoured engineer, honoured artist, honoured painter, honoured teacher, people's artist and people's painter. Such distinctions were conferred on persons who had made a major contribution to science, teaching or the arts. They were a powerful incentive for scientists, teachers and artists to excel in their work.

Notable progress in education was made every year: the numbers of schools, teachers and students increased, and educational facilities and the quality of instruction were improved. At the start of the academic year 1914/15 there were 26,100 general education schools in the Ukraine attended by 2,600,000 children, but by the academic year 1940/41 the country boasted 32,100 schools, with an attendance of 6,800,000. This made it possible to solve the increasingly complex problems in the field of education. In the early 1930s, compulsory primary education for all was introduced, and the problem of introducing universal seven-year education in rural localities and ten-year education in the cities was successfully resolved. Thus the Soviet regime solved the problem of universal education in less than two decades, whereas the officials of the old tsarist regime had estimated that it would take 100 to 150 years to achieve that objective.

A new system of instruction and education also took shape. It was based on a scientific and materialist outlook. Soviet education had a brilliant representative in the person of the educator and teacher Anton Makarenko, who developed the theory of education in and by the group and that of

20

family education. He set forth his views in *Educational Epic, Flags on Towers, A Book for Parents* and other works that achieved worldwide recognition in educational circles.

Extracurricular and out-of-school activities played an important part in the education of children, especially those carried out by the Young Communist and Pioneer organizations in Leninist assembly halls and museums attached to schools, in pioneer and student palaces, in children's clubs, at centres for young technicians and naturalists, on hikes and tourist excursions and on athletics fields. These activities brought together tens of thousands of groups which studied the life and achievements of Lenin and provided a framework for the patriotic and internationalist education of schoolchildren. To promote aesthetic education in schools and clubs, picture galleries were installed and amateur music, dance, theatre and sports groups were organized. Games and sports meetings were regularly held in schools and at district, provincial and republic levels, to show the public what such groups had achieved.

The specialized schools were also radically reorganized. Great numbers of specialists were needed for the development of the national economy, and a new national intelligentsia had to be built up which could manage the economy and see that it developed along socialist lines. Steps were immediately taken to achieve this objective. The most literate and politically conscious workers and peasants were appointed to responsible posts in the administration and economy, along with many of the old intelligentsia. At the same time, the specialized schools were reorganized so that they could train workers and the poorest peasants for highly skilled positions in all branches of the administration and economy.

In a short time a new system of specialized education had been introduced, which underwent extensive development. Whereas in the academic year 1914/15 the republic had 19 institutions of higher education, with an enrolment of 26,700 students, by 1940/41 it had 166 such institutions, with a student body of over 127,500. This expansion was accompanied by a proportionate increase in the number of trained specialists. At the beginning of 1941, 513,000 Ukrainian workers had had a secondary or higher education. They constituted the new national intelligentsia, which had come into being since the revolution. It was thanks to them that the republic developed successfully along socialist lines. In this way one of the greatest and most complex problems of the cultural revolution was solved. By the middle of the 1930s, our country no longer needed the services of foreign specialists, for it had its own intelligentsia, drawn from the ranks of the people.

In the scientific field, the primary object was to ensure that scientific personnel remained in their jobs and to reorganize scientific research activity in a manner consistent with the development of the new state. Scientific research was carried out in the departments of higher educational institutions and of the All-Ukrainian Academy of Sciences which was

21

set up by the Soviet Government in 1919. The progressive Ukrainian intelligentsia, who had longed to have their own national scientific centre, now saw their dream come true. Officially recognized as the supreme scientific institution, the Academy of Sciences was vested with responsibility for organizing the development of science in the interest of the nation and its citizens.

Among the academy's founders were men of great eminence: the historians D. Bagaliĭ and V. Peretts; the economists K. Voblyĭ and M. Ptukha (statistician and demographer); the folklore specialists and ethnographers V. Gnatyuk, A. Loboda and N. Sumtsov; the biologist N. Kashchenko; the physicist and chemist V. Kistyakovskiĭ; the philologist, orientalist and writer A. Krymskiĭ; the botanists V. Lipskiĭ and A. Fomin; and the hydrologist P. Tutkovskiĭ.

The All-Ukrainian Academy of Sciences comprised three scientific research institutes and forty-one scientific research departments, commissions, laboratories and committees, with a staff of 100 scientific workers. From the outset, it carried on the traditions of progressive scientists of the Ukraine and Russia who were dedicated to the service of the country and its people, and it set about the task of building a socialist society. State expenditure on scientific development increased from year to year, and this made it possible to expand the postgraduate training of scientific personnel, convert the research commissions and laboratories into research centres, open new research institutes and enlarge the scope of research. In 1927 the academy possessed 70 research institutions; in 1940, there were over 300 such institutions in the Ukrainian SSR, employing over 19,000 persons.

Applying Marxist-Leninist methods in their research work, scientists gained increasing knowledge of the laws governing the development of nature and society and achieved notable successes in their work. As early as 1919, the Academy of Sciences of the Ukrainian SSR set up the Commission for the Study of the Natural Resources of the Ukraine, and in 1927 the Commission for the Study of Productive Forces, which later became the Council for the Study of the Productive Forces of the Ukrainian SSR. The commission engaged scientists to carry out research on ways of developing the productive forces of the socialist economy and to draw up five-year plans for the development of the national economy. In 1936, the Institute of Economics was set up to make a scientific study of the socialist reorganization and development of the national economy and to investigate theoretical and practical problems of the economy.

Considerable progress was made in the field of Ukrainian historical studies, especially after 1936, when the Institute of Ukrainian History was established; it was staffed by young scholars who had done academic and postgraduate work in Soviet higher-education institutions. The year 1934 saw the establishment of the Institute of the History of Material Culture, which replaced the archaeological commissions and committees;

it was subsequently reorganized and became the Institute of Archaeology, which specialized in Ukrainian archaeological studies.

Research in the history of Ukrainian literature and art was done in the T. Shevchenko Institute of Literature, founded in 1926, and in the Institute of Folklore, Ethnography and the History of Art, which was established in 1936, replacing the Ethnographic Commission and the Laboratory of Musical Ethnography of the Ukrainian SSR Academy of Sciences.

The social and political changes in the life of the Ukrainian people and the development of a new way of life and culture were accompanied by the revitalization of the Ukrainian language, both in its practical aspects and as a mode of literary expression, and by the enrichment of its vocabulary and style. It was realized that linguistic studies on the evolution of the language should be undertaken and that it should become the national language. To this end, the Institute of Linguistics was established in 1921, and subsequently departments of linguistics were set up in teacher-training institutes and universities.

Ukrainian language specialists developed and introduced a new orthography and produced textbooks and manuals in Ukrainian for use in general educational and specialized secondary schools and in higher education institutions.

Considerable advances were made in the fields of mathematics, physics and chemistry. V. Vernadskiĭ, the outstanding mineralogist and chemist and first president of the All-Ukrainian Academy of Sciences, was the founder of the new science of geochemistry. World renown was achieved by the algebraic school of D. Grave and the mathematical school of N. Krylov and N. Bogolyubov, who elaborated the theory of non-linear and differential equations and non-linear variations. Universal recognition was accorded to the chemical, medical and biological schools founded by D. Zabolotnyĭ, A. Bogomolets, A. Palladin, V. Lyubimenko, V. Vorob'ev and other eminent scientists. In 1923, the country's first Institute of Labour Hygiene and Occupational Diseases was opened in Kharkov. Work in the field of the protection of mothers and children proceeded apace.

In the mid-1920s systematic studies of the geology and hydrology of the Ukrainian SSR got under way, as did research in the fields of materials and powder metallurgy.

The role played by young, Soviet-educated scientists in all branches of science became increasingly important. In 1928, the Ukrainian Physico-Technical Institute was opened in Kharkov, and it soon became one of the country's major centres of theoretical physics. In the early 1930s, four young associates of the Institute—A. Val'ter, G. Latyshev, A. Leĭpunskiĭ and K. Sinel'nikov—succeeded in splitting the atom of lithium.

In 1929, a department of structural engineering with a welding laboratory was established through the efforts of E. Paton; it subsequently became the Institute of Electric Welding. The institute's laboratory developed metal-welding techniques that were used for the first time in

23

joining major components of hydraulic structures during the building of the Dnieper hydroelectric station. In the 1930s, a team of scientists led by the well-known physicist and chemist A. Brodskiï, working in their laboratory in Dnepropetrovsk, produced the first heavy water ever obtained in the Soviet Union, an achievement of tremendous importance in the subsequent development of atomic science.

A great deal of research was done and considerable success was achieved in agricultural science—in the genetics, selection and acclimatization of plants. The studies carried out over a number of years by a team led by A. Sapegin on interspecific hybrids of soft and hard wheat gained world-wide recognition. Every year Ukrainian scientists made fresh discoveries that added to the scientific knowledge possessed by their country and by the world and did much to further the reconstruction of the national economy and the improvement of the educational, ideological and cultural level of the people.

A new literature and art, dedicated to the service of the people and the enrichment of their intellectual life, developed and prospered under the Soviet regime. The fact that the workers now enjoyed extensive rights and freedoms and could effectively exercise them was conducive to the massive development of artistic creativity.

There was a renaissance of traditional Ukrainian arts and crafts: pottery-making, embroidery, wood-carving, weaving. Skilled craftsmen drew their inspiration from the new themes of everyday life or the old themes of Ukrainian and world classical literature. The articles such craftsmen produced, apart from their utilitarian purpose, became increasingly infused with an ideological-aesthetic and didactic quality. Workshops and schools were established in many regions to promote the decorative and applied arts. Handicraft exhibitions became a regular feature of Ukrainian life as early as 1919.

The Ukraine had long been renowned for its songs and musicians, especially its kobza and bandore players, who were hounded by the authorities in prerevolutionary days. Under the Soviet regime, these ancient musical art forms have flourished. Professional and amateur choral groups and bandore ensembles have been organized. Folk-songs and traditional working-class revolutionary poetry have inspired popular songs, choruses and marches that extol the socialist transformation of the country and the joys of free collective labour brought by the victory of the collective farm system. The *kolyadki* (ritual songs) and *shchedrivki* (traditional Ukrainian folk-songs about everyday life) were a particularly rich source of inspiration for the new songs composed by simple folk-singers or by the kobza and bandore players of the present day. Wending their way freely through the towns and villages of the Ukraine, they sang the new songs and those of bygone days to their own accompaniment. In keeping with the old tradition of expressing in song their thoughts about the important happenings and events of the life of society, the kobza players composed songs and ballads

24

that rang with the new revolutionary spirit. Folk art served as a major source of inspiration for the works of professional artists.

Members of the pre-revolutionary intelligentsia used their creative powers to serve the new literature and art. They included the writers S. Vasil'chenko and N. Tereshchenko; N. Leontovich, Ya. Stepovoĭ and K. Stetsenko, who were eminent composers; the painters I. Izhakevich, G. Svetlitskiĭ and N. Samokish; men and women of the theatre like M. Zan'kovetskaya, P. Saksaganskiĭ and A. Zatyrkevich-Karpinskaya and others. But it was the young, talented writers, painters and amateur performers—workers, peasants and soldiers in the Red Army—who made up the rank and file of the new intelligentsia. They met in workshops or in centres connected with newspaper editorial offices or cultural institutions, and they formed literary, musical and art societies.

Many vicissitudes marked the development of Soviet Ukrainian literature and art; it was fraught with ideological contradictions which gave rise to bitter conflicts between diverse currents of thought. This was due partly to the influence of the forces of reaction and the partisans of the decadent and formalist schools of literature and the arts, who were faced with the sweeping changes carried out in the Ukraine after the victory of the Great October Socialist Revolution, and partly to the magnitude of the tasks assigned to literature and the arts.

The Communist Party took systematic, scientifically based action to develop the class-consciousness of writers and artists and make them aware of their responsibility towards society. It called on them to take an active part in building up a new life, while preserving all that was best and progressive in the country's cultural traditions and renewing and enriching its culture by constructive criticism. Even in the darkest years, when things were disorganized and the economy was not yet stable, the nation's publishing houses produced editions of the Ukrainian classics—the works of T. Shevchenko, I. Franko, Lesya Ukrainka, M. Kotsyubinskiĭ, Panas Mirnyĭ and others, as well as translations into Ukrainian of Russian and foreign works. At the same time, the party cautioned writers against the dangers of national exclusiveness and of conserving time-worn and obsolete ideas. It also called for constructive co-operation between national cultures and their mutual enrichment through the exchange of both cultural information and delegations, including theatrical groups and orchestras, and also recommended an increase in the number of translations.

The party also did much to organize and unite writers and artists. The best among them rallied to the cause—the service of the people, who were engaged in the building of socialism. The method they adopted for their creative work was that of socialist realism, which was based on the truthful portrayal of reality in its revolutionary development.

All the writers who were committed to the building of the new society voluntarily joined together in the Ukrainian Writers' Union. According to its statutes, adopted at the First All-Union Writers' Congress in 1934, the union is a voluntary association of writers who are participating, through their works, in the building of communism and the struggle for peace and friendship among peoples. It seeks to promote the creation of works of a high ideological and artistic standard. Membership is open to prose writers, poets, playwrights, literary critics, scriptwriters and translators who, by their writings, actively contribute to the building of communist society. Members must have published works of intrinsic artistic or scientific value.

Unions of painters, musicians and architects were organized along similar lines and are governed by the same principles.

Writers and artists drew their inspiration from the great changes in the life of society they had witnessed and in which they had played their part, and in their works they dealt with national and international events of importance that affected the life of their country.

The works of Ukrainian authors were characterized by diversity of genres, styles and artistic techniques and by the depth of interpretation and investigation of their themes; but their purpose is always to give a true account of major events in the history of the Ukrainian people and of their working lives and to demonstrate the strength of the friendship of the peoples of the Soviet Union and their love for their homeland and the Communist Party. P. Tychina, the great poet and writer of Ukrainian Soviet works, has done so with consummate skill and accuracy in his poems *The Party Leads* and *We Belong to One Family*.

Among the pioneers of Ukrainian Soviet literature we may mention especially N. Bazhan, O. Vyshnya, A. Golovko, A. Kopylenko, M. Ryl'skiĭ and V. Sosyura.

The dramatic arts became the vehicle for recording the major events in the new life that was unfolding. M. Irchan, I. Kocherga and I. Mikitenko established the reputation of the Ukrainian theatre both in the Soviet Union and abroad. In his heroic tragedy *The End of the Fleet*, the eminent playwright Aleksandr Korneĭchuk, who took an active part in public affairs, depicted the immortality and spiritual grandeur of the millions of people who were opening up a new age in the history of mankind. His play *Truth* was the first Ukrainian dramatic production to immortalize the image of V. I. Lenin, the leader of the revolution. Korneĭchuk's outstanding play *Platon Krechet* described the lofty moral and political qualities of the new Soviet intelligentsia. He produced many works dealing with significant events in the life of the Soviet people.

Advances were made in the theatrical and musical fields and in the fine arts. The success achieved in these spheres was in many ways due to a vast campaign to spread the ideas of the socialist revolution and acquaint the masses with the activities of leading personalities in history, science and culture by means of the arts. In the early days of the Soviet regime, monuments were erected in many towns and villages in memory of illustrious figures—for instance, the monuments to V. I. Lenin, Karl Marx and Taras Shevchenko in Moscow and Petrograd, and the monument to

26

the great eighteenth-century philosopher Skovoroda, in Lokhvitsa (in the Poltava region); other monuments were erected to commemorate the victory of the Revolution. In the 1930s magnificent monuments in honour of Shevchenko were erected in Kharkov, Kiev and Kanev, where he was buried.

In the fine arts, in which the painters I. Kavaleridze, V. Kasiyan, V. Kostetskiĭ, M. Lysenko, A. Petritskiĭ, A. Strakhov, K. Trokhimenko and A. Shovkunenko were outstanding, the principal works were inspired by the socialist changes made possible by the revolution.

The development of music in the Ukrainian SSR owes much to composers such as F. Kozitskiĭ, K. Boguslavskiĭ, V. Kosenko, G. Ver'ovka and M. Verikovskiĭ, who composed many choral works. Symphonic and operatic works began to appear in the mid-1920s, among them L. Revutskiĭ's great Second Symphony, B. Lyatoshinskiĭ's operas *The Golden Hoop* and *Shchors*, M. Verikovskiĭ's opera *Naĭmychka* (The Farm Girl), based on Shevchenko's poem, M. Skorul'skiĭ's *Song of the Forest* and K. Dankevich's *Lileya*, both ballets, A. Ryabov's operetta *The Fair at Sorochinsk* (adapted from Gogol) and G. Maĭboroda's symphonic poems *Lileya* and *Kamenyary*.

The works of the artist, thinker and citizen Aleksandr Dovzhenko are evidence of the high standard of Ukrainian cinematographic art. They chronicle the heroic achievements of the Ukrainians and of all the peoples of our country. In his film *Zvenigora* (1928), Dovzhenko traces the historical fate of the Ukrainian people and their march towards the revolution, and in *Arsenal* (1929) he describes the revolution itself. *Earth* (1930) was the first film that dealt with collectivization; for power of imagery and depth of poetic interpretation of the socialist transformation of the countryside, it remains unsurpassed to this day. *Ivan* (1934) dealt with the industrialization of the country and the building of the Dnieper Hydroelectric Station. *Aerograd* (1936) was concerned with the building of a new town, a defence outpost on the country's eastern frontier. One of Dovzhenko's best productions was *Shchors* (1939), which will go down in the history of the cinema as an epic portrayal of a people's struggle to bring about the triumph of Lenin's ideal—the establishment of Soviet power.

As literature and the arts progressed, greater numbers of literary works, films, musical compositions and works of art were produced. The period 1930–40 saw the production of 162 films and the publication of 7,430 literary works, including both works in Ukrainian and translations. Thus from the outset Ukrainian literature and art chronicled the heroic exploits of the men and women who brought about the socialist transformation of the country. Painters portrayed vividly and with profundity the revolutionary changes affecting the whole life of society, the emancipation of labour and its transformation into a free and creative force, which in turn had led to the development of new social phenomena, the most characteristic among them being socialist emulation on a mass scale, which Lenin had predicted.

27

Writers and artists showed how socialist emulation—comradely competition and co-operation among workers—developed the abilities of hundreds and thousands of toilers and brought out the best qualities of the new man, those of a patriot, an internationalist and an active builder of socialism.

Cultural policy had only one aim—to raise the general educational and cultural level of the workers and satisfy their rapidly growing spiritual needs. It is noteworthy that particular attention was given to the development of the information media and the organization of cultural and educational action among workers. A vast network of cultural and educational institutions was created—clubs, libraries, museums and cinemas. In 1920 there were some 15,000 such centres, but by 1940 there were over 53,000; they served as centres for spreading political and economic information, and also for the development of amateur artistic activities extolling the new life. They provided facilities for group and individual activities, for meetings and gatherings, lectures and evening discussions, talks and conferences, concerts, professional and amateur shows and film projections.

As the educational level of the population rose, more circles and schools were organized for people with an interest in history, technology, agronomy or amateur artistic activities. In January 1941 over a million persons, most of them young people, were studying in such circles, some 60,000 of which were in operation.

For the most part, these circles engaged in artistic activities—choral and instrumental music, the theatre and dancing. The members developed their talents in accordance with the best traditions of Ukrainian art, and their own art was enriched by contact with the artistic achievements of the peoples of the USSR. In this way they made a remarkable contribution to the aesthetic education of the people.

Rapid progress was made in the field of the press and book publishing. At the republic and local levels, the party, the Soviets, trade unions, the administrative authorities and youth services published newspapers in Ukrainian, Russian, Polish and other languages; industrial enterprises and collective farms began publishing large-circulation newspapers. In 1940, 1,672 newspapers with a total daily circulation of 6.9 million copies were published in the Ukraine.

Scientific, technical, academic and literary works and translations were published in large editions. In the twenty years before the revolution (1897–1917) some 1,600 titles, or an average of about eighty a year, were published in the Ukraine (and only ten or fifteen of these a year were in the Ukrainian language), but 5,430 titles appeared in Ukrainian in seven and a half years of the Soviet regime. By the end of the 1930s, 4,500 titles came out on average every year, mostly books on socio-economic and political subjects and the works of the founders of scientific communism, Marx, Engels and Lenin, which were in great demand. During the period 1918–40 close to a hundred editions of the works of Lenin appeared, totalling over 1.2 million copies. During the same period, the works of Marx and Lenin went through over forty-four editions. In the prerevolutionary period books and newspapers were a rarity in the villages; now they were readily available even in the most remote rural localities and farmsteads.

Under the Soviet regime, far-reaching changes took place in physical education and sport. In the past, few people had indulged in such things, but now they became popular with the masses. Committees on physical education and sport were formed in the provinces, towns and districts to organize such activities for the people. Physical-education groups were organized in factories, institutions, schools and villages; they carried out physical-education training programmes and athletic activities.

An organization known as 'Ready for Labour and Defence' became the backbone of the physical-education movement. It pursued the humanist aim of fostering the healthy and harmonious physical development of Soviet citizens. Amateurs of physical education and sport could use gymnasiums, stadiums, swimming-pools, athletics fields and other sports facilities without payment; in 1940 there were 14,000 such facilities. By the mid-1930s, the majority of Ukrainian youth were engaged in physical education and sport, as against a mere 9,000 persons from the ruling classes in the period before the revolution.

The development of culture in the Ukrainian SSR and the distinctive features and nature of the new culture that was growing up aroused keen interest abroad. With a view to acquainting foreign peoples with the cultural achievements of the Ukrainian people, the Society for Cultural Relations with Foreign Countries was established in the mid-1920s. It developed contacts with progressive organizations in a number of countries abroad, provided them with information on Ukrainian cultural and scientific achievements and helped Ukrainian writers and artists to take part in exhibitions held in other countries and to undertake tours abroad. The dissemination in other countries of reliable information on cultural development in the Ukraine was promoted by foreign progressives and workers' delegations who had visited the Ukrainian SSR. For example, the French writer Henri Barbusse, who played an active part in the life of his country, visited Kharkov in the autumn of 1929 at the invitation of Ukrainian writers. On returning to France, he did a great deal to inform world public opinion about Ukrainian cultural achievements.

With every passing year Ukrainian culture became more widely known in other countries. From 1922 on, the Ukrainian SSR participated in international exhibitions. At the Leipzig World Fair that same year, artists from Kharkov won the Gold Medal, the highest distinction awarded, for the special postage stamps they had designed on the theme of aid to the hungry. At the World Art Exhibition in Italy, in 1928, *The Family*, a painting by the Ukrainian artist F. Krichevskiĭ, was adjudged one of the best among those on display. The displays illustrating the successes achieved by the Ukrainian SSR in eradicating adult illiteracy and in the development of science, literature and art aroused great interest among visitors to the Cologne World Fair.

29

In 1929 the Dumka Choral Group enjoyed a tremendous success on its tour of France and won acclaim as one of the best choirs in the world. The Ukrainian films *Taras Shevchenko* and *Natalka Poltavka* were highly successful in France, Czechoslovakia, the Netherlands, the United States and Canada. Progressive American newspapers wrote that *Natalka Poltavka* gave the lie to the fascists who claimed that Ukrainian culture was dead. The film was banned in a number of cities abroad by authorities who feared its impact on the working classes.

After viewing Dovzhenko's *Arsenal*, Barbusse wrote in the Parisian weekly *Monde* that it was a 'remarkable', 'powerful' and 'passionate' film. The American critic James Leyda compared Dovzhenko's film with Picasso's 'Guernica'; he said that they were alike in their implacable hatred of violence, impassioned lyricism, ardent humanism, the fusion of the universal and the national in the deepest sense of these words, and artistic expressiveness of form.

In November 1930 the Conference of the International Bureau of Revolutionary Literature met in Kharkov; this in itself was testimony to the success of the development of Ukrainian culture. Over a hundred delegates from thirty countries took part in this literary conference. They visited industrial enterprises, schools, universities, and scientific research and cultural institutions, and everywhere they saw the enormous creative activities that were under way. The Kharkov Conference was an important international event.

By the end of the 1930s the republic had on the whole succeeded in overcoming centuries of backwardness. It now possessed its own national intelligentsia. By 1939, 88.2 per cent of the country's total population were literate, including 82.9 per cent of the female population. Out of every 1,000 members of the working population, 139 had had a higher or secondary (complete or incomplete) education; 109 of these were workers and 30 were collective farmers. The antagonism between town and country and between intellectual and physical labour had been overcome.

The new socialist culture played a vital role in the formation of the Ukrainian socialist nation. It was a new type of nation; its nature, its spiritual qualities and its political aspirations were new. It was marked by several distinctive features: Soviet patriotism and socialist internationalism, a high degree of political consciousness, an enthusiastic attitude towards labour, and fraternal friendship towards all the peoples of the USSR. As a result of the successes achieved by the land of the Soviets in the social, economic and cultural spheres, the Communist Party of the Soviet Union, at its eighteenth congress, in March 1939, could justifiably proclaim that our country had virtually completed the construction of a socialist society and begun the gradual transition to communism. The Ukrainain people harnessed all its energies and political vigour to the attainment of that goal, but its peaceful, constructive labours were interrupted by the war.

Implementation of cultural policy
during the period of socialist construction

On 22 June 1941 fascist Germany, perfidiously violating the Treaty of Non-Aggression, launched an attack on the Soviet Union. The aim of the leaders of fascist Germany was the annihilation of the first socialist state in the world. Hitler's fascists, abetted by their stooges, the Ukrainian bourgeois nationalists, advanced into the Ukrainian SSR, determined to subjugate the Ukrainian people. The destiny of our country, the future of world civilization, of progress and democracy, hinged on the outcome of the war.

Answering the call of the Communist Party, the whole Soviet nation rose to the defence of the motherland. Despite setbacks in the early part of the war, the peoples of the Soviet Union, the Ukrainians amongst them, never doubted that they would emerge triumphant. At the front and in the temporarily occupied territories, by heroic labours in the rear, by word and by song, the Ukrainian people fought valiantly against the fascist invaders. In battles against the Hitlerite aggressors and in the temporarily occupied territories, over 5,300,000 inhabitants of the Ukrainian SSR lost their lives at the hands of the fascist butchers. Over 2 million persons were driven into fascist labour camps. The fascist occupiers razed and burned to the ground nearly 30,000 towns and villages, making some 10 million people homeless; they destroyed and plundered all industrial enterprises, machine and tractor stations, collective and state farms, plants and factories, some 35,000 educational establishments and scientific and cultural institutions; they plundered museums, libraries, churches and cathedrals and destroyed a large number of priceless cultural monuments. It is estimated that the damage suffered by the Ukrainian economy at the hands of the fascist aggressors amounted to 285 thousand million roubles. The Soviet Union bore the brunt of the war, which cost it the lives of 20 million persons, but it emerged victorious.

In that war, the Soviet people won a military, political and economic victory over its enemies: it defended its homeland and saved the peoples of Europe from fascist enslavement; it gave generous support to the countries of Asia in their struggle against Japanese imperialism and saved the peoples of the whole world from the danger of fascist oppression.

As soon as the fascist invaders began evacuating Ukrainian territory in the winter of 1942/43, the local organs of state administration began functioning again and set about the task of rebuilding the national economy and cultural centres. In August 1943 the Central Committee of the Communist Party and the Soviet Government issued a special decree that prescribed a series of measures for restoring the economic and cultural life of the liberated regions. The requisite funds, building materials and equipment were made available for this purpose.

Thanks to the socialist system, the planned organization of the economy and the skilful guidance of the Communist Party, the complex task of restoring the national economy and culture was smoothly and rapidly accomplished. Two special state bodies were set up to supervise the reconstruction of the cultural infrastructure and to ensure the training

31

of qualified personnel—the Directorate for Printing and Publishing, Higher Education and Cinematography and the Committee on Cultural and Educational Activities. The latter was responsible for organizing and supervising the activities of cultural and educational institutions—clubs, libraries and museums—and for organizing lectures.

In the liberated territories the local authorities gave priority to the children and the resumption of their studies. The best of the buildings that had been spared were converted into schools. Where none had survived intact, classes were held in the hastily rebuilt ruins of old schools, in dug-outs, huts and, in the summer, in the open air. By the autumn of 1945, over 5 million children were at school—78 per cent of the pre-war figure. Schools were organized for young workers and farmers whose education had been interrupted by the war. Work was begun on the gathering of documentation about the war, and much was done for the restoration of historical and cultural monuments. In March 1943 work was begun on a museum of literature and the arts to perpetuate the memory of Taras Shevchenko, the great Ukrainian poet, artist and revolutionary democratic thinker; the T. G. Shevchenko Museum was inaugurated in 1947 in Kiev, the capital of the Ukrainian SSR.

In February 1944 the Ukrainian Government decided that the national craft industries should be revived and developed. Even before that, in September 1943, the Ukrainian National Chorus was organized with a view to fostering the development of choral and choreographic work in the Ukraine. It was led by the talented composer and conductor Grigorii Verevka, the son of a village craftsman and a pioneer in the development of choral art in the Ukraine.

From its inception, the National Chorus represented the rich and varied vocal and ethnographic regions of the Ukraine. It gave its first concerts in 1944, in the front-line regions, for the workers who were raising up Kiev from the ruins; they were an immense success. In no time, its fame spread far beyond the borders of the Ukraine, and it is now known throughout the world.

In 1944, whilst the country still lay in ruins, the Academy of Sciences, many institutions of higher education, libraries, theatres, film studios, museums, publishing houses and printing plants, which had been evacuated, returned and resumed their activities. By the close of 1945, 230,000 students were enrolled in secondary and higher educational institutions, 267 research institutes were functioning again, and the work of reconstruction was going ahead on a large scale.

In 1939, 1940 and 1946 respectively, Galicia, Bukovina and Transcarpathia, Ukrainian lands lying to the west, were reunited with the Ukrainian SSR to form a single Ukrainian Soviet state. This was a momentous event in the life of the Ukrainian people and the fulfilment of the lifelong dream of the workers of those areas, who had struggled indefatigably for unification.

group
the
-heroine,
ikhnyuk, a
f Socialist
.

chenko.]

Amateur choir in
the district of
Zmievsky,
Kharkov region.

Memorial in Kie[v]
at the Museum [of]
the History of t[he]
Great Patriotic
War of 1941–194[5]

Bogdan-Khmel'n[itsky]
Square in Kiev.

The ruthless domination of foreign colonizers had kept these regions in a state of extreme economic and cultural backwardness. Even according to official statistics, 50 per cent of the population was illiterate, and nearly 90 per cent in the rural areas of Bukovina. In the school year 1938/39 there were only 138 Ukrainian schools for the 8 million inhabitants of the Western Ukraine. The admission of Ukrainians to higher education in their own land was severely restricted, owing to the existence of a *numerus clausus* or quota, which had official sanction. As a result, Ukrainians comprised only 10 to 12 per cent of total enrolments in higher educational institutions.

After the reunification of the Western Ukraine—Bukovina and Transcarpathia—with the Ukrainian SSR, the workers in those regions were hungry for knowledge. The Soviet state provided them with the necessary funds and equipment for the schools and the scientific and cultural institutions that were now being built. Some 30,000 teachers and specialists and several thousand skilled workers, engineers and technicians were sent to these regions. They explained the nature of Soviet cultural policy and encouraged the workers to put it into effect. However, they encountered the fierce resistance of nationalist gangs and the Uniat Church, which were in the service of imperialism. Hundreds of people—ordinary workers who were helping the people to overcome their lack of education and ignorance and also people who were seeking for knowledge—fell victims to these bandits.

Cultural progress was rapid in the western provinces. By 1950, illiteracy among the adult population had been all but wiped out; all the workers' children were receiving instruction in their mother tongue.

Secondary and higher education was reorganized in existing schools and new specialized secondary and higher educational institutions were built which now, for the first time, were open to the children of workers. Not only did they pay nothing for tuition, they also received state grants. The new institutions included a State University in Uzhgorod, Medical Institutes in Chernovtsy and Ivano-Frankovsk, an Institute of Applied Arts in Lvov, and an Institute of Industrial Arts in Kosov. Cultural education schools were set up in all the provincial centres for the training of cultural leaders. Most of the students came from small towns and localities and, on completion of their studies, they returned to their home towns to build a new life.

In a short time, the western provinces were covered by an extensive network of cultural institutions, the number of which grew from year to year. During the first five years, 5,500 clubs, reading-rooms and libraries were opened in rural areas alone. Amateur artistic activities sprang up everywhere. In 1950, 24,800 amateur art groups were functioning in the villages, with the participation of 371,000 persons.

These cultural activities, together with the provision of educational facilities, led to an improvement in the cultural level of workers; ignorance became a thing of the past. Socialist ideas and new attitudes took root in the lives of the people of the western provinces and accelerated the socialist transformation of the economy. The changes that took place provided still further evidence of the truly limitless opportunities offered by the socialist system for the cultural development of workers.

Now that peace was restored, the Soviet Ukraine could give priority once again to economic organization, culture and education.

The land of the Soviets and its people returned to their peaceful and constructive labours and set about the task of completing the construction of socialism and establishing a communist society. But first the devastating effects of the war had to be overcome, and the national economy restored and developed beyond its pre-war level. The country was faced with the vital necessity of bringing about a rapid rise in the people's standard of living and satisfying their spiritual needs through the development of culture. At the same time, however, the defence capacity of the country had to be strengthened, in view of the threat of a new act of armed aggression that lurked behind the cold war unleashed by imperialist circles.

The first post-war five-year plan—the Plan for the Reconstruction and Development of the National Economy of the Ukrainian SSR for the period 1946–50—was approved in August 1946. The plan provided for the restoration of the cultural infrastructure, the introduction of universal education, a sizeable increase in the number of trained specialists for the national economy, the development of science, the expansion of the network of theatres, cinemas and cultural education institutions, and a considerable improvement in the standard of cultural work.

Workers, collective farmers and intellectuals threw themselves into the task of rebuilding the economy. By the end of 1950, it was by and large back to normal, and some branches had even surpassed their pre-war levels of production. This enabled the work of building a communist society to be tackled on an increasingly wide scale.

The amounts allocated from public funds for cultural purposes and for payments and benefits to the people rose year by year, and this made it possible to expand cultural construction and satisfy more fully the spiritual needs of the workers. Expenditure on social and cultural activities, which amounted to almost 1,135,000 roubles in 1950, exceeded 3,058,000 in 1960.

As in the past, emphasis was laid on the development of education. By 1947/48 practically all children of school age were attending school. A year later, as a result of the progress achieved, it was possible to resume the transition to universal compulsory seven-year education, which had been interrupted by the war. As industrial and cultural requirements grew, increasing numbers of skilled workers and specialists with a secondary or higher education were needed, and the general development of science became necessary.

Rapid progress was made in higher and secondary specialized education. Fifteen new higher education institutions opened their doors in the first years after the war. In the academic year 1950/51 over 160 higher educational institutions were in operation, with a student body of over 200,000. During the period 1946–60 higher and secondary specialized educational institutions turned out 812,200 specialists for the national economy and the cultural sector. The number of specialists with a higher or secondary school education working in the national economy rapidly increased, totalling 1,661,000 persons in 1960.

By the beginning of 1948, the network of research institutes had been restored and considerably expanded. The country's scientists themselves took part in the rebuilding of the various branches of the economy. Group methods were more widely used in research, and this accelerated the study of large-scale and complex subjects.

The Academy of Sciences of the Ukrainian SSR, in collaboration with the Academies of Sciences of the USSR and the Byelorussian SSR, studied problems concerning the use of water-power resources and the drainage and irrigation of large tracts of land, and it also carried out research in nuclear physics. Theoretical research was carried out successfully in radiophysics and electronics, calculus mathematics, mechanics and the chemistry of high-molecular compounds and of non-ferrous and rare metals.

Ukrainian scientists, working in collaboration with scientists of the rest of the country, contributed to studies on the peaceful use of atomic energy and the development and launching of artificial satellites and space rockets. Worldwide recognition has been accorded to the works of Academician N. Bogolyubov in mathematics, I. Frantsevich in physical metallurgy, K. Sinel'nikov in biochemistry, V. Gutyrya in chemistry, V. Filatov in ophthalmology and N. Strazhesko in therapeutics. Soviet Ukrainian scientists have achieved notable successes in the development of computers. In the early 1950s, a team led by Academician S. Lebedev developed and produced the first electronic calculator in the USSR and in continental Europe. Thus the foundations were laid for the Ukrainian school of cybernetics, which, under the direction of Academician V. Glushkov, has won recognition both at home and abroad.

Progress was made in the agricultural sciences. New, more productive varieties of wheat, barley and sugar-beet were introduced. Particularly remarkable work was done by the scientific institutes headed by V. Yur'ev, F. Kirichenko, I. Buzanov and B. Sokolov. The varieties they developed were used on millions of hectares of land in our country and many countries abroad. Agricultural scientists did much to improve crop yields.

Scholars pursued their studies of Ukrainian history, philosophy, the history of the state, the history of law, Ukrainian literature, folklore, ethnography, linguistics and socialist economic development. In the social sciences, increasing attention was given to questions concerning the theory of socialism and the interpretation of historic experiment of the building of socialism and its worldwide role.

The intensive development of science speeded up the progress of the revolution in science and technology, which produced qualitative changes in the production process and led to the wide-scale introduction of mechanization and automation. By the mid-1950s agriculture was almost entirely mechanized, and most rural areas were supplied with electricity.

Such changes necessitated a rapid improvement in the cultural and technical level of workers, collective farmers, engineers and technicians. In the mid-1950s, practically half of the workers in the industrial labour force were taking some kind of technical training programme at schools teaching modern working methods, technical training courses, schools providing evening and correspondence courses in general educational subjects, technical schools or institutes. In 1956 over 700,000 workers obtained higher qualifications than they had had previously, and over half a million workers acquired new skills by training on the job. The training of machine operators and other specialists for agriculture got under way. Between 1953 and 1956, 515,000 skilled agricultural workers were recruited.

The development of the scientific and technological revolution made new demands on the general educational and specialized schools. Action was therefore taken to improve the quality of instruction at all levels of the education system and throughout the cultural network. The government consulted the working masses on the question, as on all other state matters of great importance. In 1958, draft proposals 'on strengthening the links between the school and life and on the further development of education in the country' were drawn up and thrown open to nationwide discussion. In April 1959, the Supreme Soviet of the USSR adopted a law to this effect, which was based on the principle that general education should be integrated with polytechnical education.

The Great Patriotic War confirmed the profound social significance of Soviet literature and art. The beauty of the Soviet personality produced by the socialist system was revealed in all its grandeur during the Great Patriotic War against the fascist aggressors and became an inexhaustible source of inspiration for writers and artists. The main theme of post-war literature and art was the struggle for peace and friendship among peoples. Such themes as the glorification of the age-old friendship between the Ukrainian people, the Russian people and the other peoples of our country and the role of Lenin and the Communist Party in forging the unity of the peoples are appropriately dealt with in almost every work of any importance. The theme of work also became a *leitmotiv* of literature and art. Man the creator, dedicated to the welfare of his homeland and the maintenance of peace throughout the world, endowed with high moral qualities in his public and personal life and infused with spiritual grandeur, is the hero of most artistic and literary works.

Ukrainian literature and art produced large numbers of works of consummate artistry, inspired by lofty ideological principles, that have enriched the treasure-house of national and world culture. Alongside members of the older generation, writers like L. Pervomaĭskiĭ and A. Malyshko

36

and painters like S. Grigor'ev, M. Deregus and S. Shishko rose to prominence; and new talents emerged on the literary scene: Oles' Gonchar, M. Stel'makh, P. Voron'ko, S. Oleĭnik, P. Zagrebel'nyĭ and N. Oleĭnik. Writers from the western Ukraine have joined their ranks, men like P. Kozlanyuk and Yu. Mel'nichuk; painters like I. Bokshaĭ and O. Kul'chitskaya, the composer S. Lyudkevich and others as well. Among the hundreds of works of literature and art, the following may be mentioned: the dramatic works *The Grove of White Hazel Trees* and *Makar Dibrova*, by A. Korneĭchuk, *Under the Golden Eagle*, by Ya. Galan, *Prague is Still Mine*, by Yu. Buryakovskiĭ; the operas *Bogdan Khmel'nitskiĭ* and *Nazar Stodolya*, by K. Dan'kevich, *The Young Guard*, by Yu. Meĭtus, *Milana*, *Arsenal* and *Taras Shevchenko*, by G. Maĭboroda; the ballet *Song of the Forest*, by V. Kireĭko; the symphonic poems *Grazhina* and *On the Banks of the Vistula*, by B. Lyatoshinskiĭ, and *Armenian Sketches*, by A. Shtogarenko; the paintings *The Young Taras Shevchenko Visiting the Artist K. Bryullov*, by G. Melikhov, *The Masters of the Earth*, by A. Maksimenko, *Bread*, by T. Yablonskaya, *The Return*, by V. Kostetskiĭ, *The Black Sea Folk*, by V. Puzyr'kov; the films *Feat of a Scout* (1947), by B. Barnet, *Taras Shevchenko* (1951), by I. Savchenko, *Spring on Zarechnaya Street* (1956), by F. Mariner and M. Khutsiev, and many others. Ukrainian literature and art achieved greater maturity and diversity of genre, style and form.

The number of original titles and translations of works by authors from other Soviet republics or from abroad published in the Ukrainian SSR, increased from year to year. The number of titles of fiction rose from 211 in 1946 to 599 (including 456 in Ukrainian) in 1950. The network of theatres expanded, more film studios were built, and film production grew; retrospective, thematic or commemorative art exhibitions and film festivals were held every year.

Literature and art developed, reaching an increasingly high standard, and works of exceptional quality were produced which became part of the cultural life of the peoples and contributed further to their education. Such works were greatly admired by the Ukrainians and other peoples of the USSR and enjoyed the esteem of all progressive people.

The press, book publishing, radio and television occupied a prominent place in cultural activities, as can be seen from the following figures. In 1946, 2,151 titles were published in editions totalling 44 million copies; in 1950, 4,236 titles in editions totalling over 77.5 million copies. In 1946, 884 general political or specialized newspapers were published at the national or local level, with an overall circulation of 3.5 million copies; in 1950, 1,192 such newspapers were published with a circulation in excess of 4.6 million copies.

Around 1950, 1,500,000 radio receivers connected with group networks and 68,500 individual receivers were operating in the country, the broadcasts being in Ukrainian, Russian and Hungarian.

Old museums were renovated and new ones built, the most important among them being the Kiev branch of the V. I. Lenin Museum and a new branch of the same museum in Lvov. They play an important part in familiarizing workers with Lenin's ideas. In 1958 there were 124 museums—historical and commemorative museums, museums of regional studies and art museums—in the Ukrainian SSR. Amateur ethnographers have set up many museums and display rooms, which are staffed by voluntary workers.

Over the years the network of clubs spread, their activities becoming more and more diversified. Thousands of Red Corners were organized in factories, workers' hostels, house management offices and collective farm team centres. Every day the workers took part in various social activities organized by clubs or at Red Corners. Here they participated in meetings celebrating an important event of the past or present, and they could attend lectures on current events, talk to a party activist, read newspapers or see a film or an amateur show. Here were the people's universities and polytechnic, technical and artistic circles. Amateur art exhibitions, reviews and contests were organized to draw people's attention to the achievements of amateur artists and to develop new national talent.

The network of public libraries grew, and the standard of their work improved. In 1958, the republic boasted some 34,000 libraries, with 170 million books on their shelves. In terms of numbers, cultural and educational establishments in the Ukrainian SSR occupied second place in the world.

Great attention was devoted to the question of patriotic and internationalist education. Almost every locality had its memorial or monument to perpetuate the memory of heroes who had fallen in the fight against the fascist aggressors. Anniversary celebrations were arranged in honour of outstanding persons in the nation's history and in culture, and were widely observed.

The development of socialist culture after the war was accompanied by a rapid rise in the educational, cultural and technical level of the workers, as it was in the pre-war period. In 1959, 99.1 per cent of the republic's population was literate. Moreover, 456 out of every 1,000 workers and 244 out of every 1,000 collective farmers of the country's total labour force had had a higher or secondary (complete or incomplete) education. At the beginning of 1959, the intelligentsia comprised some 3.7 million persons, 1.5 times more than in 1939. It was therefore possible to adopt new targets for the cultural policy and to attain its final goal—the full and harmonious development of the personality.

Implementation
of cultural policy
during the period
of advanced socialism

During the period of the transition from socialism to communism, the land of the Soviets was faced with the task of creating the infrastructure of communism, developing communist relationships in society and training the new man—a human being who possessed great spiritual qualities and moral purity and who also had an excellent physique.

The cultural development of the people in the period of the all-out effort to build a communist society is the final stage in the great cultural revolution. For, in the final analysis, almost everything else depends on it: the increase in the productive forces of the economy, technological progress and the organization of production, the growth of the social activity of the workers, the development of the democratic foundations of self-management and the communist reorganization of the whole way of life.

Communist culture, which assimilates and develops all that is best in world culture, will be a new and higher stage in mankind's cultural development. It will embody the spiritual life of society in all its diversity and richness, the lofty moral substance and humanism of a new world. It will be the culture of a classless society, the culture of all the people and all mankind.

The concluding phase of the cultural revolution takes place in a period of accelerating scientific and technological advance accompanied by qualitative changes in production and in the nature and organization of work. It was therefore indispensable to raise the educational, cultural, technical, ideological and political level of the people as a whole even more rapidly, especially that of the rising generations, by providing secondary education for all, expanding and improving the training of skilled workers and specialists for the national economy, enlarging the scale of scientific research work and fundamentally reorganizing cultural and educational activities.

Under these circumstances cultural questions acquire even more importance, a fact reflected in the decisions of Communist Party congresses and

39

in the five-year plans for the development of the national economy. Every five-year plan marks a new step forward in economic and cultural development. The tenth five-year plan, whose goals were laid down by the twenty-fifth Congress of the CPSU and the twenty-fifth Congress of the Communist Party of the Ukrainian SSR, gave special importance to cultural development.

In accordance with the decisions of the congresses, efforts are directed towards the implementation of certain specific tasks: the scale of cultural development, introducing universal secondary education, improving the quality of education and specialist training, fostering the development of science, and satisfying more fully the spiritual needs of the people. These efforts are supported by a broad-based programme of action under which improvements of various kinds are being introduced—the rational organization of the housing sector, the establishment of a network of community and cultural centres and the development of means of communication and transport, thus providing workers with satisfactory living and working conditions and opportunities for study and relaxation.

As before, the Soviet state plays the major role in the implementation of cultural policy and the further development and improvement of socialist culture. The cultural progress of the workers, the lofty level of their spiritual aspirations and the increasing role of the spiritual factor in the building of communism are fostered by the constitution, which increases and enhances the functions of the state as an organizer of cultural and educational activities and also broadens the rights and duties of workers in the realm of cultural life. Under advanced socialism, the constitution accords a much larger place than in the past to provisions dealing with the state of spiritual life in Soviet society and defining the various functions of the state as well as the rights and duties of citizens and of public organizations.

For the first time, the constitution includes a special chapter on social development and culture, which contains provisions reflecting the cultural achievements of socialism and the policy of the state in the three main areas of cultural progress—education, science and the arts. Other important aspects of the cultural life of the people and of the cultural strategy of the Ukrainian state are dealt with in other sections of the constitution.

The task of directing the development of science and culture is carried out by the highest organs of state power and administration of the Ukrainian SSR, namely the legislative body—the Supreme Soviet of the Ukrainian SSR and its Presidium—and the executive body—the Council of Ministers of the Ukrainian SSR and its ministries and departments. At the local level, the Councils of People's Deputies and their executive committees are in charge of cultural affairs. They are assisted by Standing Commissions on Cultural Affairs which organize and supervise cultural construction.

The Ministry of Education of the Ukrainian SSR is responsible for the development of general secondary education and for pre-school and out-of-school education. It operates through the education departments of the executive committees of the local Soviets of People's Deputies in each province, city, district and village. The Ukrainian SSR State Committee for Vocational and Technical Education is responsible for vocational and technical education. Higher and secondary specialized education is the responsibility of the Ministry of Higher and Secondary Specialized Education. The activities of cultural institutions and establishments providing instruction in cultural subjects and in art are directed by the Ministry of Culture of the Ukrainian SSR. Press and publishing, television, radio and films are supervised by state committees.

In accordance with the constitution of the Ukrainian SSR, the state organs collaborate closely with public organizations—trade unions, the Komsomol, the unions of writers, composers, painters, architects and film workers, and various volunteer associations like the Association of Knowledge, the Association for the Safeguarding of Historical and Cultural Monuments, the Association for Environmental Protection, and others. Over the years, many of these associations have become mass organizations bringing together millions of workers, and they have acquired considerable experience. For example, Ukrainian trade unions have a membership of some 25 million, the Komsomol brings together over 6.5 million boys and girls, and the Association for Knowledge has a membership of close to 10 million.

The steady, rapid growth of the economy has made it possible to increase expenditure on cultural development. Expenditure on education and science in 1970 amounted to 1,866 million roubles, but by 1978 it reached 4,226 million roubles. This has made it possible to expand and improve the infrastructure of scientific and cultural institutions.

The increased part played by the state in the management of cultural construction, and also improved planning and better financing have a powerful impact on cultural progress under socialism and on the creation of the intellectual conditions necessary for the transition to communism.

Education

Under the conditions of advanced socialism, as before, education is one of the principal problems that must be tackled by the cultural policy, for education lies at the heart of cultural development The progress made in education and the prospects for its further development are set out in full in the constitution of the Ukrainian SSR, Article 25 of which states: 'In the Ukrainian SSR, there is a single education system, which is being constantly improved; it provides general education and vocational training for citizens, gives young people a communist upbringing, promotes their physical development and trains them for work and social activity.' The system covers pre-school education, general secondary education, out-of-school education, vocational and technical education, secondary specialized education and higher education.

The country is now in a position to ensure that all citizens have access to the education system. The constitution guarantees them the right to pursue their studies and to develop all the aspects of their personalities. Article 43 of the constitution of the Ukrainian SSR declares that citizens of the republic have the right to education. This right is guaranteed in practice by various provisions: education of all types is free, secondary education is universal and compulsory for young people, and there are all sorts of opportunities for vocational and technical training, and for secondary specialized and higher education, which is linked to life and to production. Besides all this, students can take correspondence courses and evening classes, they are entitled to state grants and benefits, textbooks are obtainable free of charge, students may choose their mother tongue as the language of instruction, and facilities are provided for independent study.

The socialist educational system is based on democratic and humanistic principles that are established by law. By virtue of the law on education, all citizens have the right to education irrespective of race and nationality, sex, religion, property status and social status; education is compulsory for all children; all educational institutions are run by the state; pupils may choose the language of instruction; all types of education are free of charge; the education system is unified, and in all types of educational institutions students can progress from one level to the next; all children and adolescents follow the same course of studies and are educated in a communist spirit; the education of the rising generation is linked with life and with practical work for the building of communism; education is scientific and communist in character and is based on high moral principles; schools are co-educational; education is secular and free of all religious influence.

The aim of education is to produce well-educated people, with harmoniously developed personalities, who are active builders of communist society, people reared on Marxist and Leninist ideas and brought up to respect Soviet laws and socialist law and order, people who have a positive attitude towards work, who are physically healthy and capable of taking an active part in social and state activities and who are prepared to defend their socialist homeland selflessly, to preserve and increase its material and spiritual wealth and to protect and safeguard nature.

The development of education is ensured by the steady expansion of the network of pre-school and school establishments and improvements in their equipment. During the period 1961–75 alone, 10,000 new schools were built in the Ukraine, over 8,000 of them in rural localities. Nearly one-fifth of village schoolchildren were attending new schools. The new schools have excellent facilities, large, bright classrooms, study-rooms, laboratories, workshops, gymnasiums and refectories. Over the same period, the number of kindergartens and nurseries increased to 22,000, and the number of out-of-school establishments—Young Pioneer Palaces, centres for young technicians and naturalists, excursion and tourist centres, children's parks, stadiums and pioneer camps—rose to 10,500.

Much has been done to ensure that schools are located rationally, in places where they are most readily accessible to pupils. At the same time, the school network has been reorganized, the number of general secondary schools being increased and the number of primary and eight-year schools decreased.

Pre-school education, the first link in the Soviet educational system, is the object of special concern on the part of the state. It is carried out in nursery schools, kindergartens, playgrounds and pre-school centres, which are open to children from the age of two months to seven years. The staff of these pre-school institutions work in close collaboration with the family to ensure the harmonious mental and physical development of the children and prepare them for the day they enter school; at the same time, they make it possible for mothers to take an active part in the social and economic life of the country.

Article 51 of the constitution of the Ukrainian SSR reads:

The state shows its solicitude for the family by providing and developing a broad network of child-care institutions, by organizing and improving communal services and public catering, by paying grants on the birth of a child, by providing children's allowances and benefits for large families and also family allowances and assistance of other kinds.

In 1980 one out of every two children in the republic was attending a pre-school institution. It is expected that in the near future all children will be covered by the pre-school education system.

The general secondary school is the backbone of the educational system. It provides a general vocational and polytechnic education for youngsters from 7 to 17, over a period of ten years (classes 1 to 10). In the school year 1979/80, there were 23,400 schools of general education attended by 7.5 million pupils—that is, all children of school age. The teachers totalled 456,500.

In accordance with the tenth five-year plan for education, special attention is being given to the introduction of universal compulsory secondary education for adolescents and to the improvement of the education provided. During the period 1966–76, the content of secondary school education was thoroughly reorganized and improved through the introduction of new methods of teaching which were intended to stimulate the independent cognitive activity of the pupils and to help them think for themselves and apply the knowledge they had acquired. Thus education was enabled to cope with the needs of scientific and technological progress.

The system of teaching in specially equipped rooms, which enables studies to be combined with practical work, has been introduced into practically all secondary schools and nearly half of the eight-year schools, in order to increase the effectiveness of education. Moreover, vocational education has been improved. Notable improvements have also been made in out-of-school education, which is intended to supplement and deepen the knowledge students acquire in school and to encourage them to play an active part in community life. It is carried out in Young Pioneer Palaces for pioneers and schoolchildren, in centres for young technicians and naturalists, at excursion and tourist centres, in sports schools for children and teenagers, in children's parks and elsewhere. Most schools and out-of-school institutions have Lenin museums or rooms, museums commemorating the heroic achievements of the revolution, the army and the workers, regional studies museums and international friendship clubs. There are tens of thousands of young naturalists' and technicians' societies, choral, music and drama groups and other groups attached to schools and out-of-school institutions. Seventeen thousand well-equipped gymnasiums and sports complexes are available for the physical training of pioneers and schoolchildren.

During the summer, children go to pioneer camps for health and relaxation, to work and rest-camps (where they do light work four hours a day), to sanatoriums and children's homes; more of such facilities are made available every year. In 1980, they totalled 25,500 and provided rest and recreation and a healthy environment for over 5 million children and teenagers.

One aspect of the reorganization of the work of secondary schools was the improvement of the system for the pre-service and in-service training of teachers. Teacher training is carried out in nine universities, thirty teacher-training institutes and forty-six teacher-training schools. During the period 1976–80 they trained over 162,000 teachers for schools of general education. The republic now has an efficient system for the in-service training of teachers, by means of which they can improve their teaching skills and general proficiency.

Improving the working and living conditions of teachers is a constant concern of the state. Teacher's Day is celebrated annually. Teachers play an active part in the social and political life of the republic, a fact which fosters the development of their civic spirit. Many of them have become prominent educators, for instance Vasiliĭ Sukhomlinskiĭ, a man of peasant stock, who began his career as a village schoolteacher in Kirovograd Province.

Sukhomlinskiĭ has expounded his pedagogical views in a number of scholarly works, among them *I Give My Heart to the Children (Serdtse otdayu detyam)*. Published in 1969, this book soon achieved worldwide recognition among people in the teaching profession and was awarded the State Prize of the Ukrainian SSR. For his noteworthy contribution to the study of the theory and methodology of communist training, both in schools and at home, the all-round development of the pupil's personality and the art of teaching and for his action is disseminating information about the humanistic principles underlying Soviet pedagogy. V. Sukhomlinskiĭ received the titles of Honoured Teacher of the Ukrainian SSR and Hero of Socialist Labour. In recognition of his scientific activity, he was elected a Corresponding Member of the Academy of Pedagogical Sciences of the USSR.

The Ukrainian people are constantly achieving greater successes in the development of education. In the school year 1978/79, 99.1 per cent of all pupils in schools of general education received a secondary education. Thus one of the major objectives in the field of education—universal compulsory secondary education—was attained. The schools train pupils satisfactorily for entrance to higher educational institutions—the children of working-class parents, collective farmers and defenders of the socialist motherland. At the same time, in view of the accelerated tempo of scientific and technological progress, the change-over of the economy to intensive development and the speeding up of cultural development, every effort is being made to improve the quality of education and of the vocational and moral training of the pupils, to strengthen the links between education and life and to train pupils more effectively to do socially useful work.

The system of vocational and technical training has been improved so as to meet the needs of the national economy and the demands of scientific and technological progress. The range of specialized studies has been broadened, and better curricula and study programmes have been introduced. The network of vocational and technical schools is constantly being extended. In 1966, 700 were in operation, and they had a student body of 285,900; in 1980, they totalled over 1,000, their student body had risen to 723,000 and they offered some 600 different courses. In the 1970s vocational and technical schools were established mainly on the basis of the secondary schools (complete programme). Students in vocational and technical schools pay no tuition fees, and increasing numbers of them are entirely supported by the state.

Vocational and technical schools have trained over 10 million workers since they were first set up. At present, 25 to 35 per cent of the industrial labour force are trained in these schools. Distinguished by their technical competence and broad general knowledge, they worthily perpetuate the heroic traditions of the working class.

In the period of advanced socialism, as in the period of socialist construction, specialized education has developed according to a plan. The scope of specialist training has been broadened to meet the new demands of the economy, and the work of educational institutions has been reorganized to ensure the high quality of such training.

In the academic year 1979/80, there were 870 specialized educational institutions in the Ukrainian SSR which trained over 1.6 million citizens of the republic. Over twenty new institutions of this kind were established between the late 1950s and 1979. Today, every provincial centre has its own higher and secondary specialized institutions. Between 1960 and 1980, the number of students per 10,000 of the population rose from 97 to 196. Over the same period, the educational institutions in question offered courses in over 100 new subjects.

The infrastructure of these educational institutions has been markedly strengthened, and the material situation of both students and teachers has been much improved. Almost all students receive state grants, and those who did not live in the locality where the institution is are housed in hostels.

There has been a steady increase in the size of the staff in specialized educational institutions. In 1959, higher education institutions employed 23,200 teachers, over 9,000 of whom held academic degrees; in 1970, they employed some 55,800, 48.7 per cent of whom held academic degrees. A carefully planned, effective system for improving the professional level and performance of staff members is in operation.

Most higher education institutions are large, well-equipped educational complexes. In pre-revolutionary Ukraine the total enrolments in all institutions of higher education were about 35,000; today, one such institution, in the Kiev Polytechnic Institute, has approximately the same number of students.

The results of these improvements in the system and quality of specialist training are increasingly noticeable. Increasing numbers of specialists are trained at secondary schools and higher educational institutions and are qualified for work in all branches of the national economy and culture. During the seventh five-year plan (1961–65), higher and secondary specialized educational institutions trained 861,200 qualified specialists, during the ninth five-year plan (1971–75), 1,740,700, and during the tenth five-year plan, 1,924,000. In 1980, over 18 million persons were pursuing studies of one kind or another; 84 per cent of the working population had had either a higher or a secondary (complete or incomplete) education.

Scientific development

As we know, science today plays an increasingly important role in the life of a nation. Article 26 of the constitution of the Ukrainian SSR lays down the main lines of the state's management of scientific activity and outlines future policy in that domain. It reads: 'In accordance with society's needs, the state makes arrangements for the planned development of science and the training of scientific personnel and sees that the results of research are applied to the economy and other spheres of life.'

The scientific potential of the Ukrainian SSR is growing and expanding. Today, as in the past, the Academy of Sciences, higher educational institutions and specialized research and industrial design centres are the mainstay of scientific activity.

Higher educational institutions, the universities in particular, have a large number of highly qualified scientific workers and teachers and excellent facilities at their disposal. In 1977, Ukrainian higher educational institutions had over 70,000 such specialists on their staffs, more than 25,000 of whom were directly engaged in scientific work.

Scientific research in these institutions is conducted in laboratories that deal with a particular problem or field, in scientific research institutes and departments, in astronomical observatories and botanical gardens and in faculty departments. The scope and pace of research work are increasing every year. During the period 1971–75, higher educational institutions completed over 20,000 scientific projects, 4,900 more than in the previous five-year period. In the course of the ninth five-year plan, 15 scientific studies carried out in institutions of higher education were awarded state prizes.

The Academy of Sciences is the major centre of scientific activity in the Ukraine today, as it was in the past. In 1980, it co-ordinated the activities of over 80 scientific institutes, employing some 70,000 persons, 300 of whom were Members or Corresponding Members of the Academy and over 7,000 Doctors or Candidates of Sciences. In the Ukraine as a whole, the

the
ians, an
artistic
e in
tsy
e.
V. Landar.]

Marriage on a
collective farm in
the village of
Verguny,
Cherkassy Province.
[*Photo*:
G. Kaminskiĭ.]

Palace of Culture
in Kiev.

Monument to the
Unknown Soldier,
Kiev.

number of scientific workers increased from 94,000 in 1965 to roughly 189,000 in 1979, including 60,700 Doctors or Masters (Candidates) of Science. In the same period over 100 new scientific research institutes were established, among them the Institutes of Low Temperature Physics and Technology, Geophysics, Cybernetics, Semiconductors, Radio Engineering, Mechanical Engineering, Physical-Organic and Organic Chemistry, of Cryobiology and Cryomedicine, Molecular Biology and Genetics, State and Law, and the Economic and Social Problems of Foreign Countries.

The location of research institutions was improved; they were set up in proximity to industrial sites. A number of major scientific centres were established to co-ordinate the research activities of institutes attached to the academy, those concerned with a particular problem, and higher educational establishments. Apart from Kiev, Kharkov and Lvov, where such centres already existed, new ones were created in Donetsk, Dnepropetrovsk, Simferopol, Sebastopol and Odessa.

The Academy of Sciences of the Ukrainian SSR gives priority to the development of fundamental research, applied research and experimental design projects. It places the emphasis on the development of long-term integrated research subjects enlisting the combined efforts of its own scientific institutes, higher educational establishments and administrative departments of the country and other republics and often of those in other socialist countries.

Together with the co-operative agreements concluded between scientific institutions and enterprises, new and more effective forms of collaboration are becoming more common, for instance collaboration between a scientific research institute and a particular branch of production, or within a major scientific and technical complex, embracing institutes attached to the academy, scientific and research institutes affiliated with higher educational institutions, design bureaux, experimental production enterprises and bodies not financed by the state. The study of major multidisciplinary or integrated problems is carried out through the combined efforts of various scientific institutes, enterprises and departments.

Under the tenth five-year plan, the research institutes of the Academy of Sciences of the Ukrainian SSR, in co-operation with various ministries and departments, are engaged in research on 19 multidisciplinary themes; they are carrying out 440 studies for different branches of industry and are working on nearly 1,500 other projects and 90 major programmes of national interest.

This system of research makes it possible to tackle important multidisciplinary problems, which often means that new fields of scientific investigation are opened up, new technologies are developed and marked improvements are made in labour productivity and the quality of production; it also leads to radical changes in whole branches of production and to the development of new branches. Between 1970 and 1975 some 5,000 new machines, machine-parts, instruments and apparatus were produced thanks to the efforts of scientists.

In the course of the tenth five-year plan, over 11,000 scientific innovations have been introduced each year, with resultant gains to the national economy of over 1,500 million roubles.

Ukrainian scientists are making new discoveries all the time. In the field of mathematics applied to mechanical engineering, a prominent role is played by the Institute of Cybernetics, headed by A cademician V. Glushkov, a Hero of Socialist Labour and Lenin Prize w nner. The theory of digital automation, elaborated by scientists of this[1] institute, provided the basis for the development of various types of computers and control machinery now in use, such as the 'Kiev' digital machines and the 'Dnieper', 'Promin' ('Luch'), 'Mir' and 'Mir-2' control machines (the country's first such machines), which measure up to top world standards. For the first time ever, the institute put forward the idea of increasing the intelligence of machines, which it carried through in practice. It is also working on the development and introduction of automatic systems for the control of production.

Studies are going forward in the fields of nuclear physics, solid-state physics, low-temperature physics, radiophysics, the physics of semiconductors, theoretical physics and electronics. Kharkov scientists developed one of the world's largest radio telescopes and the largest of existing electronic accelerators, both of which are now in service. Ukrainian specialists studying the world's oceans discovered a new current in the Atlantic, which has been named the Lomonosov Current in honour of the great Russian scientist. Pioneering work is under way in the field of experimental space oceanography.

The Institute of the Physics of Metals of the Academy of Sciences of the Ukrainian SSR has a leading position in world science, as a result of its achievements in the study of metals and alloys. Valuable work is being done in the field of powder metallurgy. In a short time scientists have created over 500 different types of cermets that possess remarkable properties (they support heavy loads and resist high temperatures); they are being successfully introduced into many new branches of industry, as well as traditional ones. The Institute for the Study of Materials of the Academy of Sciences of the Ukrainian SSR, which deals with theoretical aspects of the problems of materials, is the country's leading authority in the field and has won worldwide recognition.

As in the past, a prominent place in world science in the field of the welding of metals is occupied by the E. Paton Institute, headed by the President of the Academy of Sciences of the Ukrainian SSR, B. Paton, who has been twice honoured as a Hero of Socialist Labour. Apart from its many outstanding achievements—fifteen have been awarded the Lenin Prize and State Prizes of the Ukrainian SSR and the USSR—it has made a notable contribution to space welding techniques. The Institute has developed techniques and highly reliable equipment for welding in space which were used for the first time ever in 1969 on the space ship Soyuz.

Other major scientific and technological achievements of Ukrainian scientists are the theoretical elaboration and development of techniques for producing extra-hard metals and artificial diamonds for industrial use and the manufacture of high-speed cutting tools.

Scientific planning has also resulted in tremendous successes in technology, biology and medicine. We shall mention but a few examples of the successes achieved in agriculture.

A team of scientists in the Mironovka Scientific Research Institute for Wheat Selection and Seed Growing (Kiev Province), headed by Academician V. Remeslo, a Lenin Prize winner and twice named a Hero of Socialist Labour, has developed a large number of high-yield varieties of wheat and other cereals. These varieties are used on almost one-third of the country's sowing area and have resulted in additional crop yields whose value runs to thousands of millions of roubles. Mironovka varieties of wheat are also sown in a number of countries of Europe, Asia and America.

Valuable work is also being done by the All-Union Selection and Genetic Institutes and by other institutes concerned with agriculture, irrigation, the sugar industry, agricultural economics and organization, etc. The application of their achievements has brought about a radical transformation of agriculture, resulting in improved efficiency, greater yields per hectare and greater interest on the part of farmers, whose labour has become more meaningful and creative.

Let us now turn to the social sciences, a field in which an enormous contribution is being made by historians, philosophers, economists and specialists in literature, the arts, language and the law.

Several important works have been published, among them the seventeen-volume *Ukrainian Soviet Encyclopedia*, the first Ukrainian encyclopedia ever published; the *Soviet Encyclopedia of Ukrainian History*; such basic works as the *History of the Ukrainian SSR*, in a two-volume and an eight-volume edition; the *Victory of the Great October Socialist Revolution in the Ukraine*, in three volumes; the *Ukrainian SSR during the Great Patriotic War of the Soviet Union (1941–1945)*, in three volumes; the *History of State and Law in the Ukrainian SSR*; and the *Triumph of Leninist Philosophic Ideas in the Ukraine*. Basic works on the history of the working class and peasantry and on Ukrainian cultural development have also been published: the *History of Ukrainian Literature*, in eight volumes and the *History of Ukrainian Art*, in six volumes, the latter of which was awarded the State Prize of the Ukrainian SSR in 1971.

The Ukrainian language, which is in use in all spheres of public life, has flourished and become richer. Having developed, in the course of its history, from the vernacular of the Middle Dnieper region and, after the unification of all the Ukrainian lands into a single socialist state, having assimilated the most characteristic features of the linguistic groups of the

Ukrainian ethnolinguistic area, modern Ukrainian as a literary language is the most valuable cultural possession of the Ukrainian people.

The school of Ukrainian linguistics has produced a number of basic works elucidating the grammatical structure, the vocabulary, syntactical perfection and diversity of the Ukrainian language, its history, its historical dialects and its contacts with the languages of other peoples of the Soviet Union and of the Slav world. Among the best known and most widely used works, the following should be mentioned: *Ukrainian Orthography (Ukraïns'kiĭ pravopis)*, the code of rules governing the spelling of the modern literary language; one-, two- and five-volume courses on modern literary Ukrainian; one- and two-volume courses on the history of literary Ukrainian; courses on the historical grammar and dialectology of the Ukrainian language; a large number of dictionaries, including a two-volume *Glossary of the Language of T. G. Shevchenko (Slovnik movi T. G. Shevchenko)* and twenty or so dictionaries of specialized terms.

In all these works the study and interpretation of the history of the Ukrainian language in its organic relationship with the history of the people, their social life and their contribution to the construction of socialism is based on a scientific conception, as is the understanding of the social and aesthetic evolution of the language and its capacity to apprehend and transmit all the new notions thrown up by socialist and communist construction.

The achievements of scholars in the field of linguistics help to accelerate scientific and technological progress, the development of the national economy and culture, the raising of the educational and cultural level of workers and the country's advance towards communism.

Both the government and the people greatly appreciate the contribution made by scholars to the motherland. For outstanding services to science, over 400 of them have been awarded the Lenin Prize and state prizes. Forty-nine have been honoured as Heroes of Socialist Labour; five of them have received this title twice.

Literature and art
in the life of society

In the period of advanced socialism, tremendous progress has been made in literature and the arts. As the constitution of the Ukrainian SSR states (Article 27), everything is done in the republic to encourage professional and popular creative work in these fields.

The work of writers and artists and the activities of their unions are influenced by important events in the social and political life of the people and of the country more than by anything else. Writers and artists are profoundly moved by everything that concerns the Ukrainian people—their thoughts and aspirations, pride in their heroic past, their efforts to preserve peace. The heroic times we live in, action in favour of communism, the life of the working community, in which the most noble of human aspirations are embodied and the civic character of all who are involved in the building of a new life is moulded—these have become the dominant themes of literature and art.

In addition to the pioneers of Ukrainian Soviet literature who brought it into the mainstream of world literature, there is now a new generation of writers who are committed to the building of communism through their work and to fostering high moral standards among Soviet people. It includes writers like B. Oleĭnik, I. Drach, V. Zemlyak, V. Simonenko, Yu. Mushketik, V. Korotich and others too numerous to mention.

The new works, which are found in increasing numbers in bookshop and libraries, are palpable evidence of their authors' desire to play an active part in the life of society, to study it exhaustively, to assimilate the rich material that our age provides and to arrive at a philosophical interpretation of the world today in relation to the cultural and intellectual progress of Soviet society. Writers are seeking new forms and genres, new styles and ways of writing by which to portray human characters in all their profundity.

The main characteristics of the new literature are optimism, humanism, the affirmation of truth and justice, the glorification of friendship among peoples, and faith in the triumph of peace and in a radiant future for all mankind. The works of Ukrainian writers are published in over forty languages of the peoples of the USSR and also in dozens of foreign countries, where they are appreciated by men of good will.

This flowering of literature is having a good effect on the development of all the arts—the theatre, music, the fine arts, films and popular art; they are imbued with ideological principles and a lofty aesthetic sense of purpose, while they continue to perpetuate and enhance the classical legacy.

Besides long-established theatres like the I. Franko Academy of Ukrainian Dramatic Arts in Kiev, the T. Shevchenko Theatre in Kharkov, the M. Zan'kovetskaya Theatre in Lvov and the Lesya Ukrainka Theatre of Russian Drama in Kiev, which have all been honoured by the highest governmental awards, new lyrical and dramatic theatres have been founded in Vinnitsa, Ternopol, Zaporozh'e, Chernovtsy and other provincial centres and are adding their contribution to the flowering of Ukrainian theatrical art.

These theatres stage Ukrainian, Russian and foreign plays, both classical and modern. Modern plays are the most popular; they account for 70 per cent of all performances. In many theatres contemporary problems are dealt with and the heroes of our time are portrayed in innovative psychological and philosophical dramas like *Pages from a Diary* and *The Heart Remembers*, by A. Korneĭchuk, which, as the audiences realized, were profound, poetic meditations on the value and creative potential of the human personality during the period of advanced socialism and on the lofty aspirations of Soviet man—worker, patriot and internationalist.

In *The Paths We are Choosing*, based on a play by N. Zarudnyĭ, in *Savage Angel* by A. Kolomiĭts, and in *Hullo, Pripyat*, by A. Levada, we find contemporary man, with all his qualities—zeal for work, breadth of political thought, high moral standards and richness of spirit. The plays of P. Zagrebel'nyĭ, L. Dmiterko and M. Stel'makh are in the same vein.

The opera and ballet are thriving. Ukrainian operas and ballets—*Bogdan Khmel'nitskiĭ* and *Nazar Stodolya*, by K. Dan'kevich, *Milan*, *Arsenal*, *Taras Shevchenko* and *Yaroslav the Wise*, by G. Maĭboroda, *The Young Guard*, *Stolen Happiness*, *The Ul'yanov Brothers* and *Richard Sorge*, by Yu. Meĭtus, *Ten Days that Shook the World*, by M. Karminskiĭ, *Through Flame* and *The End of the Fleet*, by V. Gubarenko, and *The Awakening*, by L. Kolodub—are staged in many opera-houses throughout the Soviet Union.

A particularly noteworthy aspect of Ukrainian cultural life is the ballet, in which composers such as K. Dan'kevich, V. Gomolyaka and M. Skorik have won renown, and also musical comedy, by composers such as A. Filippenko, Ya. Tseglyar, V. Il'in, I. Poklad and others.

Soviet music has made its mark in all spheres of creative work and interpretation. It is marked by its profound assimilation and original use of folk music and also by its mastery of modern techniques of musical expression. The classical traditions of Ukrainian musical art have been further developed by L. Revutskiĭ and B. Lyatoshinskiĭ.

Ukrainian composers have produced a number of artistically outstanding symphonies, cantatas, oratorios, instrumental pieces and songs dedicated to the Revolution, the exploits of Soviet workers, the friendship of peoples—which Lenin supported—and the international solidarity of working people. Their works reflect the grandeur of our times and embody a profound philosophical interpretation of the principal problems of our day. Examples of such works are I. Shamo's Third 'Kiev' Symphony, G. Taranov's *Three Monuments*, a symphonic poem dedicated to the memory of those who fell during the Great Patriotic War, A. Shtogarenko's Fifth and Sixth Symphonies, L. Kolodub's First and Second 'Carpathian' Rhapsodies, E. Stankovich's Third Symphony 'I Proclaim' and the choral works of A. Bilash, L. Dychko and P. Maĭboroda, to mention only a few.

The Seventh Congress of Ukrainian Composers, which met in Kiev in April 1979, provided evidence of the great successes achieved in music and the broad thematic and stylistic range of the exploratory work done by Ukrainian composers. Over 150 recent works—symphonies, cantatas, oratorios, instrumental pieces, popular songs and ballads—by over 100 composers were performed by the best ensembles and soloists. The success achieved in symphonic music is evidence of the growing musical culture of the Ukrainian people.

The diversity of dramatic and musical works contributes to the development of actors and opera singers. Only a few years ago an opera-house and ballet theatre was opened in Dnepropetrovsk; in no time, it won recognition for the professional quality of its performances. The consummate skill of People's Artists of the USSR like N. Uzhviĭ, a Hero of Socialist Labour, E. Ponomarenko, O. Kusenko, V. Dal'skiĭ, A. Rogovtseva, B. Romanitskiĭ and V. Dobrovol'skiĭ; and of opera singers like D. Gnatyuk, E. Miroshnichenko, D. Petrinenko and A. Solov'yanenko, among others, is famous far beyond the borders of the Ukrainian SSR.

The theatre and opera enjoy enormous popularity, and so the state does everything possible to encourage their development. At the present time, there are eighty-two theatres in the country, including the Dnepropetrovsk Theatre of Opera and Ballet, the Theatre for the Young Spectator in Zaporozh'e, the Theatre of Drama and Comedy and the young peoples' Druzhba Theatre in Kiev, all of recent date.

Lovers of instrumental music and song have at their disposal twenty-five philharmonic societies and a travelling orchestra that performs in different parts of the country. Apart from the world-renowned State Academic Symphony Orchestra of the Ukrainian SSR, the State Academic Dumka Chorus, the Bandore Orchestra, the P. Virskiĭ State Dance Ensemble of the Ukrainian SSR, the G. Verevka State Academic Ukrainian National Chorus, all of which have been honoured by the state, a number of other orchestras and ensembles are actively promoting musical and choreographical culture in the Ukraine, including eight symphony orchestras, state brass bands and light symphony orchestras, the Kiev Folk Instrument Orchestra, the Kiev Male Chorus, the Kiev Chamber-Music Vocal Ensemble, the Bukovina, Gutsuly, Poles'e, Transcarpathian, Cherkassy and Volyn People's Choruses, the Trembita Choir, the N. Lysenko String Quartet, various instrumental ensembles, the Ukrainian Ballet on Ice and many others.

The various branches of the visual arts are progressing: painting, sculpture, and the graphic and decorative arts. The most ancient artistic traditions—the portrayal of the life of the people, its feelings, its longings and spiritual aspirations—have been developed and enriched. The theme of work and of man as a creator is the main subject of the artist's attention; it finds expression in many canvases dealing with productive labour, in portraits of Heroes of Socialist Labour and in industrial and collective-farm landscapes.

Artists of different schools are united by a common ideology, and in their works they seek to portray the realities of our life. The portraits painted by M. Bozhiĭ and A. Shovkunenko and N. Glushchenko's landscapes are distinguished by a keen sense of observation.

Motifs of great humanism are to be found in the canvases of T. Yablonskaya, People's Artist of the Ukrainian SSR, for instance in such paintings as *Bread, Nameless Heights* and *Flax*, centred around the themes of work, love, motherhood and human happiness. The works of V. Kasiyan, A. Pashchenko, V. Litvinenko, L. Levitskiĭ, G. Yakutovich and V. Chekanyuk are distinguished by freshness of theme, picturesqueness of composition, sobriety and restraint.

One of the dominant themes in Ukrainian painting is the heroic struggle of the Ukrainian people against the fascist aggressors. A. Konstantinopol'skiĭ's *Native Soil* and A. Lopukhov's *Victory* are outstanding examples of such paintings.

A number of monumental works of sculpture celebrate the valour of the Soviet Armed Forces—for example, the monument erected in Lvov, the work of the sculptors D. Krvavich, Z. Mis'ko, Ya. Motyka and A. Pirozhkov and the architects M. Vendzekhovich and O. Ogranevich; *The Ukraine to its Liberators*, a monument in the village of Melovo (Voroshilovgrad Province) where the liberation of the Ukrainian SSR from fascist occupation began, the work of the sculptors V. Mukhin, I. Ovcharenko, V. Fedchenko and I. Chumak and the architects G. Golovchenko, A. Egorov and I. Min'ko; and another monument of the same name erected near Uzhgorod, where the liberation of the Ukrainian SSR was completed; it is the work of the sculptors I. and V. Znoba and the architects A. Snitsarev and O. Stukalov.

Among the monuments erected to honour Lenin's memory in recent years, the statue in Donetsk, the work of the sculptor É. Kuntsevich and the architects N. Ivanchenko and V. Ivanchenkov, should be mentioned. The monument to the Great October Socialist Revolution in the centre of Kiev is extremely expressive; it is the work of the sculptors V. Borodaï and I. and V. Znoba and the architects A. Malinovsky and N. Skibitskiï. The monument to T. Shevchenko that stands in Moscow is the work of the Ukrainian sculptors M. Gritsyuk, Yu. Sin'kevich and A. Fuzhenko and the architect Yu. Chekanyuk, and the monument to Pushkin, in Kiev, is the work of the sculptor A. Kovalev and the architect V. Gnezdilov. These works, which are full of inner dynamism and vigour, have become the symbol of the eternal and indestructible friendship of the Ukrainian and Russian peoples. Special mention should be made of the monument to Lesya Ukraïnka in Kiev and the monument to a young Soviet soldier, Vasiliï Porik, a Ukrainian and a hero of the French Resistance, erected in the town of Hénin-Liétard (France); both are the work of the sculptor G. Kal'chenko and the architect A. Ignashchenko (the second monument in collaboration with V. Znoba).

The film industry occupies an important place in Ukrainian cultural life. There are five film studios in the country: the Kiev and Odessa Art Film Studios, the Kiev Popular Science Film Studio, the Ukrainian News and Documentary Film Studio and the Ukrtelefilm Studio. Every year they produce hundreds of feature films, newsreels and documentaries, popular science films, shorts, educational films and others. The country has over 27,000 film projectors and thousands of viewing rooms and clubs where films are shown and a great deal of educational work, of an ideological and aesthetic nature, is done.

Film directors like T. Levchuk, N. Mashchenko, V. Denisenko, L. Osyka, Yu. Il'enko, G. Kokhan and many others are following in the footsteps of the great masters of the Ukrainian Soviet cinema, A. Dovzhenko and I. Savchenko, and are working with great originality. The Ukrainian film industry has won acclaim both at home and abroad for its lofty humanism and innovative spirit. Over 200 Ukrainian feature films, popular science films, newsreels and documentaries have received international prizes, among them L. Lukov's *Great Life*, A. Alov's and V. Naumov's *Pavel Korchagin*, M. Donskoï's *Rainbow*, B. Ivchenko's *Annychka*, E. Matveev's *Postal Romance*, L. Bykov's *Only 'Greybeards' Go into Battle* and the television serials *How Steel was Tempered*, by N. Mashchenko and *Born of the Revolution* by G. Kokhan. Dovzhenko's *Earth* is considered one of the twelve best films of all time produced by any country.

Writers, composers, artists and film directors have created many brilliant works that have made their way to the hearts of the people and enriched national and world culture. Such works have won repute not only among the Ukrainian people but among all the peoples of the Soviet Union and indeed among progressively-minded people everywhere, and are a factor of great importance in the ideological and aesthetic education of the masses.

57

Writers, artists and performers are loved and esteemed for their noble service to the people from whom they themselves have sprung. They are elected to the highest organs of state administration. Persons eminent in the world of Ukrainian Soviet culture like Pavlo Tychina, Mikola Bazhan, Yuriĭ Smolich, Aleksandr Korneĭchuk, Oles' Gonchar, Mikhail Stel'makh, Vasiliĭ Kasiyan and Nataliya Uzhviĭ have been honoured as Heroes of Socialist Labour. Writers and artists receive the highest governmental awards, orders, medals and certificates of honour.

In 1961, in conjunction with the hundredth anniversary of the death of Shevchenko, the Government of the Ukrainian SSR established the T. G. Shevchenko State Prize, awarded each year for outstanding work in literature, art, architecture and journalism. Since that time, the prize has been awarded to 178 writers, artists and architects. Alongside the names of the first recipients of the prize, luminaries of Ukrainian culture, stand those of the writers P. Zagrebel'nyĭ, G. Tyutyunnik and D. Pavlychko, the composers P. Maĭboroda and I. Shamo and many others. A large number of works of literature and art have been awarded the Lenin Prize and the State Prizes of the USSR.

Popular art

In close association with the professional arts, amateur artistic activities have made steady headway in many fields—music, choral singing, the theatre, the dance, decorative and applied arts, films and photography. Amateur art activities receive generous support from the state and public organizations, and they are enjoyed by the masses. Workers, collective farmers, teachers, doctors, engineers and scientists coming from all strata and groups of the population engage in such activities, which meet high ideological and artistic standards of both creativity and performance.

The Ukrainian SSR boasts over 20,000 amateur choral groups and bandore ensembles, some 30,000 theatrical groups and tens of thousands of amateur art groups of all kinds. The Amateur People's Choir of the village of Russkaya Polyana (Cherkassy Province) grew out of the society organized by the peasantry in 1918. People of different ages and occupations sing in the choir—tractor drivers, nurses, milkmaids, young people and old-age pensioners—whose repertoire consists of popular songs and works written by professional songwriters, folk-music collected and adapted by the members of the choral group, regional melodies, lyrical and ceremonial songs, and spring songs.

For many years now, the choir of the village of Kirdana (Zhitomir Province), under the direction of O. Dobakhova, a former scout in the Partisans and retired collective-farm worker, has been deservedly famous. Its repertoire, which is well known not only at home but far beyond the country's borders—in India, Canada and elsewhere—includes folk-songs of Poles'e and new songs about village life today. There are thousands of such amateur choral groups throughout the country.

The repertoire of the Bandore Ensemble, formed in Poltava in 1947, includes Ukrainian folk-songs, songs of the fraternal Soviet peoples and songs from the world classical repertoire. For its services to national amateur art and to the cultural life and aesthetic education of workers, the ensemble was awarded the title of Honoured Amateur Choir of the Ukrainian SSR.

There are many kinds of amateur theatrical art: drama and lyric drama, opera and ballet, comedy and operetta, satire and sketches, puppet shows and young people's theatre, recitations, vaudeville, poetry readings and others. The theatrical repertoire includes dramas, comedies, tragicomedies, vaudeville shows, historical and epic plays and children's tales.

In the amateur theatres, besides variety entertainments—the one-act plays that constitute the main fare of amateur theatres—more classical plays and sophisticated works by modern playwrights are making their way into the repertoire. The best theatrical groups have put on excellent performances of Ukrainian classical and modern works, attesting to a growing mastery of staging and acting techniques and of theatrical production in general. Examples are the production of N. Kulish's play *97*, by the people's theatre at the Rovno Municipal House of Culture, the production of C. Aïtmatov's play *A Mother's Field* by the people's theatre of the House of Culture attached to the Azovstal factory at Zhdanov, and the production of A. Makaenko's play *Tribunal* by the theatre of the Palace of Culture at the Novaya Kakhovka (Kherson Province), to mention only a few.

Amateur theatre groups have a varied repertoire; thanks to their intelligence and hard work, their admirers, fellow-workers and compatriots have a chance to see all sorts of scenes from life. Amateur theatres put on thousands of shows every year for the entertainment of hundreds of thousands of people.

Relatively new forms of amateur artistic activity are catching on, such as amateur film clubs, vocal and instrumental ensembles, symphony orchestras, and groups for opera, ballet and circus work.

The most recent activity to emerge is that of amateur film-making. At the beginning of the 1970s there were about 1,350 amateur film studios in the Ukrainian SSR. Amateur films are of various types: newsreels and documentaries, popular science films, comic films and cartoons. Amateurs make films about the creative achievements of contemporary people, the heroes of the Great Patriotic War, friendship between peoples and the beauty of their native regions. Amateur film art is linked directly with life and is close to the masses. A few amateur film studios have produced dozens of documentaries (for example, that of the Chemists' Palace of Culture in Sverdlovsk), several series of films on the life of a collective-farm village (made by the Kolos Film Studio, in the district centre of Bershad', Vinnitsa Province). Since it began work in 1962, the Poles'e Amateur Film Studio in the Zhitomir area has produced some two hundred documentaries of various types, twenty of which have been awarded gold or silver medals and certificates at national, All-Union and international contests, in particular at the Montreal World Fair, Expo-67, and at the Prague and Varna Film Festivals.

Further progress has been made in the realm of the decorative and applied arts: folk painting, weaving, embroidery, ceramics, wood carving and ornamental glass-making and also in decorative wall painting, metal-work and inlaid work. Over 30,000 master craftsmen ply their trades, and nearly 50,000 work together in workshops attached to clubs.

A number of skilled craftsmen have achieved national recognition, among them mural painters like T. Pata, E. Belokur and M. Primachenko, wood-carvers like P. Verna, Ya. Khalbudnyĭ, I. Gonchar, D. Golovko, E. Zheleznyak and P. Tsvilyk, and weavers and carpet-makers like M. Vovk, S. Nechiporenko, S. Dzhus, L. Tovstukha and N. Babenko. For outstanding achievements in the field of Ukrainian applied arts—embroidery, weaving, decorative wall painting—G. Vasilashchuk, G. Veres and M. Primachenko were awarded the T. G. Shevchenko State Prize of the Ukrainian SSR. The fine ceramics produced in the village of Oposhnya (Poltava Province) and the town of Vasil'kov (Kiev Province) and the woodwork done in Kosov (Ivano-Frankovskaya Province) and Kremenchug (Poltava Province) are renowned in many countries.

Folk-art is of a high standard, and constitutes an inexhaustible source of inspiration for all culture, to which it gives its distinctive national character. It is becoming increasingly difficult to draw the line between amateur art and professional art. Many of the works of amateur composers and singers, in particular those of I. Sleta and I. Berdnik, A. Pashkevich and D. Lutsenko, P. Protsko and I. Rebro, have made their way into the repertoire of professional groups. The G. Verevka Ukrainian National Chorus, the Gutsuly and Bukovina Song and Dance Ensembles, the Lenok Poles'e Chorus in the Zhitomir Province and the Transcarpathian, Cherkassy and Volynskiĭ National Choruses all had their beginnings as amateur groups. People's Artists who began as members of amateur groups include E. Miroshnichenko, A. Solov'yanenko, D. Gnatyuk and M. Kondratyuk, all People's Artists of the USSR; A. Avdievskiĭ, E. Kolesnik, P. Muravskiĭ, M. Stefyuk and G. Tsipola, all People's Artists of the Ukrainian SSR; and M. Grinishin, Professor at the A. Korneĭchuk State Institute of Culture, A. Zagrebel'nyĭ, Honoured Artist of the Republic, and many others also began their careers in amateur groups.

Today there are 260,000 amateur art groups of one kind or another with a membership of over 7 million adults, teenagers and children—that is, almost one out of every seven inhabitants of the republic. More than 130 persons out of every thousand country-people take part in some artistic activity. Every year amateur art groups give 700,000 concerts and perform-ances, audience figures totalling almost 400 million. As has been noted by V. V. Shcherbitskiĭ, a member of the Politburo of the Central Committee of the CPSU and First Secretary of the Central Committee of the Communist Party of the Ukrainian SSR, 'The amateur art activities of the masses help to bring workers into contact with the treasures of the mind and develop healthy ideological and artistic tastes and aesthetic interests.'

The dissemination of culture

In promoting cultural development, the Ukrainian Soviet state does everything it can to ensure that the cultural wealth thus created becomes the property of the people. Article 27 of the constitution of the Ukrainian SSR reads as follows: 'The state sees to the protection and expansion of cultural wealth and its use on a large scale for the moral and aesthetic education of the Soviet people and for the improvement of their cultural standard.' A great deal of attention is therefore devoted to developing the means for disseminating culture, providing the people with newspapers, books, television and radios and organizing cultural and educational activities for them.

The Ukraine has twenty-six publishing houses, including The Higher School (*Vysshaya shkola*) and Soviet Education (*Radyans'ka osvita*), which publish textbooks, teachers' manuals, scientific and pedagogical literature and reference works for schools of general education and specialized educational institutions, Engineering (*Tekhnika*), The Builder (*Budivel'nik*) and Harvest (*Urozhaĭ*), which publish specialized technical literature dealing with building, architecture, communal housing, agriculture and forestry; Health (*Zdorov'e*), which publishes literature on medicine, health care and hygiene, physical education, sport and social security; Soviet Writing (*Radyans'kiĭ pismennik*), Dnieper (*Dnipro*) and Youth (*Molod'*), which publish the works of Ukrainian writers and translations; Festive Song (*Veselka*), which publishes children's books; Art (*Mistetstvo*) and Musical Ukraine (*Muzichna Ukraïna*), which specialize in literature dealing with art—the fine arts, amateur artistic activities, aesthetics, regional studies and travel, and Soviet and foreign music; and Scientific Thought (*Naukova dumka*), which publishes books on the various branches of science, popular science and other subjects.

The head editorial office of the Ukrainian Soviet Encyclopedia also acts as a publishing house, putting out encyclopedias and dictionaries. There are also seven multi-purpose publishing houses in Ukrainian provincial centres.

The number of titles published and the total number of copies printed are increasing every year. At present, 8,000 to 9,000 books or booklets appear annually in editions totalling between 155 and 160 million copies. Some 2,000 newspapers and journals and other periodicals are published. Over three-quarters of all printed matter is in Ukrainian.

An extensive network of libraries is provided, to ensure that books reach the widest possible public. Altogether there are 65,000 libraries: general public libraries, specialized and science libraries, departmental libraries and children's libraries, whose holdings total 760 million volumes. They are used regularly, free of charge, by 38 million readers.

The books, newspapers and magazines published are known for their accuracy, scientific reliability and great humanism, and this has won for them the confidence and esteem of their readers. Today, 980 out of every 1,000 members of the working population are newspaper subscribers. It is not for nothing that our country is often called the most book-loving country in the world, and its people the greatest readers.

Remarkable successes have been achieved in television and broadcasting. Almost everybody in the Ukrainian SSR owns a radio and television set. The country's workers have at their disposal tens of thousands of cultural and educational institutions, including over 26,000 Palaces and Houses of Culture and clubs, 162 state museums and over 3,000 museums run by public organizations, hundreds of Parks of Culture and Rest, over 58,500 Red Corners in factory shops, field stations and livestock farms, where work is constantly carried out for the ideological, vocational and aesthetic education of workers and cultural activities are organized during their free time. On the average, every club organizes around 140 educational and recreational events and 40 concerts a year for the people, in which hundreds of thousands of people take part.

The widespread dissemination of culture is also fostered by state policy, which regulates the price of admission to theatres, museums, exhibitions, cinemas and concerts. Theatre tickets cost between one and two roubles, cinema tickets, between 30 kopecks and one rouble (depending on the number of sessions attended), and the price of admission to museums and art exhibitions is 10 to 20 kopecks. The average monthly wage of workers and employees amounts to 168 roubles, 50 kopecks and that of collective farmers is roughly the same, so the purchase of such tickets hardly makes a dent in the family budget. This goes a long way to explain the enormous popularity of the theatre, the cinema and museums among all categories of the population, in particular the rural population.

Thus, the population of the Ukrainian SSR has increasingly wide opportunities to satisfy its intellectual needs.

The republic is rich in ancient historical and cultural monuments. One still finds on its territory Scythian tumuli dating back to between the eighth and fifth centuries B.C.; vestiges of the so-called Snake Ramparts—remarkable examples of fortification art—which date back to the first centuries A.D. and stretch over hundreds of kilometres in the central part of the country; the remains of the ancient cities of Olviya (Olbia), Panticapeum and Chersonese; architectural monuments of the Middle Ages—the Cathedral of Saint Sophia, the Monastery of the Caves and the Vydubitskiĭ Monastery in Kiev; monuments in Chernigov, Kamenets-Podolsk, Lvov and elsewhere. Today, over 47,000 historical archaeological monuments, sites of ancient cities and monuments of art are under state protection. The state and the people are anxious that these monuments should be preserved, thus enriching the nation's cultural heritage. In 1978, the government adopted a special law on the protection and use of historic and cultural monuments, which emphasizes that such monuments are to be used to promote the development of science and the national culture, as well as the patriotic, ideological, moral, aesthetic and internationalist education of the people. The constitution provides that public organizations, artistic associations, scientific societies and private individuals should take an active part in efforts to identify, register, protect, use and restore monuments and to disseminate information about them.

The Ukrainian Society for the Protection of Historical and Cultural Monuments, which was organized in 1966, plays a most important role in this matter. It has a membership of 14 million. It fosters the active and direct participation of broad sectors of the population in the protection of monuments, the safeguarding and use of which are under public supervision. The society is concerned with a wide variety of spheres, fundamental studies being carried out, on a voluntary basis, by different sections, dealing with the history of the pre-Soviet period, the October Revolution and Civil War, the building of socialism and communism, the Great Patriotic War, science and technology, monumental, figurative and decorative art, ethnography, town planning and architecture, archaeology, linguistic, literary, archival and documentary materials, educational work among children and young people, music and museums.

In collaboration with the Academy of Sciences of the Ukrainian SSR, members of the society take an active part in the study and preservation of historic and cultural monuments. It has organized 400 People's Universities and maintains 3,000 lecture halls and film-projection rooms, and it conducts excursions to historical sites. In co-operation with Znanie, a society for the promotion of knowledge, it publishes works dealing with problems of present-day importance concerning the history and protection of monuments. It produces numbers of commemorative badges and souvenirs for the purpose of spreading information about Ukrainian historical events and monuments. Using its own resources, the society has erected or restored statues and monuments. In Kiev, for example, it is now building a Museum of National Architecture and Ethnography, a Museum of the History of the Great Patriotic War, and others as well.

The people are particularly attached to the memory of the country's heroic past, which is bound up with the struggle for independence and for

64

social and national liberation. Over 1,300 monuments perpetuate the memory of events connected with the triumph of the socialist system, including the imposing monument to the victory of the Great October Socialist Revolution, in Kiev, and the monument commemorating the proclamation of Soviet power in the Ukraine, in Kharkov.

The military prowess of the Soviet people and their heroic labours during the Great Patriotic War against fascism have become part of history for all time. Thirty bronze busts of persons who were twice designated heroes of the Soviet Union and over 27,000 monuments and statues throughout the Ukraine perpetuate the memory of those heroic days: for instance, the magnificent monuments *Everlasting Glory* in Kiev, Odessa, Sebastopol, Kerch, Lvov, Poltava, Kharkov and Lutsk and the *Young Guard* memorial in Krasnodon. In 1976, in Kiev, at the site of Babiï Yar—the scene of a tragedy which, like those of Katyn, Salaspilsse, Lidice, Auschwitz and Dachau, is known to the whole world—a monument was erected to honour the memory of 150,000 Soviet citizens and prisoners of war who were shot by the fascist murderers. In 1980, a memorial was erected in the village of Kortelesa (Volynskaya Province) to perpetuate the memory of villagers shot by the fascist occupiers.

The people revere the memory of persons who have been eminent in culture and learning. Dozens of monuments have been erected in the republic in their honour—for example, the monuments to T. Shevchenko in Morintsy, his birthplace; to the eminent humanist G. Skovoroda; to I. Kotlyarevskiĭ, author of the first classic of Ukrainian literature; to N. Lysenko, the founder of the Ukrainian classical school of music, in Kiev; and to I. Franko, the writer and scholar, in Lvov.

A striking example of the Ukrainian people's reverence for their history is the commemoration of the fifteen-hundredth anniversary of the founding of Kiev, held in 1982. From ancient times Kiev played an important role in the history of the East Slavic tribes. In the ninth century, Kiev became the 'capital' of the ancient Russian state, Kiev Rus'. The East Slavic tribes that settled on this territory commingled with the ancient Russian people, and there gradually emerged three fraternal peoples, Ukrainian, Russian and Byelorussian, each having its own language, culture and way of life. Kiev played an important role in all the subsequent history of the Ukrainian people and its emergence as a nation, contributing to the development of its culture and its struggle for social and national liberation. At present, Kiev is a major administrative, industrial, scientific and cultural centre. It has sixty-one higher and secondary educational institutions, over thirty vocational and technical schools, some three hundred schools of general education, hundreds of pre-school establishments, seven theatres, over a hundred Palaces and Houses of Culture, hundreds of libraries, and many other cultural and educational institutions; it is also the seat of the Presidium of the Academy of Sciences of the Ukrainian SSR and of an imposing number of scientific-research institutes. Film studios and the main book, newspaper and periodical publishing-houses are also to be found in Kiev.

The restoration of the many monuments in Kiev is proceeding apace. The city has over 1,600 monuments and commemorative plaques. Apart from those already mentioned, there are monuments to Vladimir, who introduced Christianity into ancient Russia, to Bogdan Khmel'nitskiǐ, the hero of the Ukrainian people's liberation struggle for the unification of the Ukraine with Russia, and to V. Primakov, N. Shchors and V. Bozhenko, heroes of the Civil War. Over a hundred monuments and commemorative plaques perpetuate the memory of soldiers and officers who fought valiantly against the fascist occupiers and lost their lives in battle. New memorial plaques, tablets and sculptures have been placed at points of historic interest in the city. A series of works on the history of Kiev is in the process of publication; medals, badges, insignia, stamps and other objects commemorating the 1982 anniversary have also been issued.

The strengthening of cultural ties and co-operation between the Ukrainian SSR, the fraternal Soviet republics and the socialist states and their peoples has always been a major factor in the steady development and advance of Ukrainian culture. It is facilitated in particular by the fact that the countries concerned have a unified socialist economic and political system, based on Marxist-Leninist ideology, which provides the foundation for their socialist cultural development. Various events are arranged to promote co-operation between Ukrainian culture and art and the fraternal culture and art of the other peoples of the Soviet Union—literature and art festivals, held concurrently in all Soviet republics and lasting a day, a week or ten days, which give citizens an opportunity to become acquainted with the cultural achievements of the other peoples; tours by various artistic groups; and theatre festivals. Annual festivals like Kiev Spring, Crimean Dawn and Young Voices (an arts festival) have become national events, bringing together Ukrainian professional and amateur troupes as well as troupes and performers from the fraternal Soviet republics. An effective way of acquainting workers with the cultural achievements, way of life and history of kindred peoples is the celebration of the anniversaries of outstanding figures of culture like Pushkin, Lermontov, Gorky, Shota Rustaveli and others. Other Soviet republics celebrate the anniversaries of outstanding figures of Ukrainian culture like Taras Shevchenko—the watchword being 'in a new, free family'—Lesya Ukraïnka, Ivan Franko and others. Such events take place in a festive setting; they have a lasting effect, and further the mutual enrichment and international status of national cultures.

Translations are a vital factor in the whole process of cultural unification. The works of Ukrainian writers are translated into forty-five languages of the peoples of the USSR, while the works of authors representing ninety peoples and nationalities of the USSR have been translated into Ukrainian.

66

The achievements of the Ukrainian SSR in the economic sphere and in culture, education and health care are viewed with increasing interest abroad. One of the republic's principal organizations designed to satisfy such interest is the Ukrainian Society for Friendship and Cultural Relations with Foreign Countries. Established over a half century ago, it has become a vast public organization co-ordinating the activities of branches of Soviet societies for friendship with foreign countries in the provinces, cities and regions and those of affiliates and local organizations which maintain regular contact with the public at large in over one hundred foreign countries. Numbers of state, social, artistic and scientific organizations and institutions take part in the day-to-day work of the society. Its membership includes academics and schoolchildren, ministers and workers, writers and collective farmers, students and painters.

In recent years the society has organized major events abroad: Soviet Culture Days, Weeks and Months, friendship evenings, exhibitions and film festivals, which have done much to further the cause of friendship between peoples and the relaxation of international tension. In conjunction with such events, the society sends abroad representative delegations, specialized tourist groups, lecturers, painters, the best professional and amateur groups, art exhibitions of both fine arts and popular decorative and applied arts, photographic exhibitions, films, fiction and other literature and publicity and documentary information in foreign languages. At the same time, the citizens of the republic have welcomed guests from many countries of the world and have attended exhibitions of the works of artists from Portugal, Argentina, the United States, Italy and elsewhere.

The society maintains particularly close relations with the peoples of the socialist countries, on the basis of the principles of socialist internationalism. Through its affiliates and kindred associations of the Union of Soviet Societies for Friendship and Cultural Relations with Foreign Countries, the Ukrainian Society takes part in the work of a number of international organizations. It is also in close contact with the Ukrainian National Committee for Unesco and makes an important contribution to many Unesco activities.

The Ukrainian SSR attaches great importance to international cultural exchange. It does everything possible to ensure that the cultural and artistic heritage of other countries and peoples is more widely accessible to its own people. Under an efficient exchange system, it organizes a variety of exhibitions by foreign artists, music and theatre festivals and film shows, and is active in book publishing and translation. The expansion and strengthening of cultural relations with foreign countries is an important aspect of Ukrainian cultural policy. The cultural policy is carried out in accordance with the basic decisions adopted by Unesco in that field, including the provisions of the Declaration of the Principles of International Cultural Co-operation, the Recommendation concerning the International Exchange of Cultural Property, the Recommendation on Participation by the People at Large in Cultural Life and their Contribution to it, and in conformity with the principles of the Final Act of the Conference on Security and Co-operation in Europe. The Ukrainian SSR fully supports all forms of international cultural exchange, which it regards as an aspect of international co-operation that is of great importance for the strengthening of peace and détente and of friendship and mutual understanding among peoples.

Conclusion

In fraternal co-operation with the peoples of the USSR, the Ukrainian people has consistently pursued a scientifically planned cultural policy, and since the establishment of the Soviet regime it has achieved notable successes in developing a truly national culture. Cultural life is vigorous; cultural values are being enriched, the system for the dissemination and use of cultural values is being improved, the network of cultural, artistic and educational institutions is being expanded, and the quality of the moral and humanistic climate of intellectual life is improving. Everything possible is done to strengthen the unity of cultural life, socialist ideology and a scientific outlook on the world, and to see that these principles are deeply ingrained in the minds of the people. All this contributes to the rapid rise in the general cultural and technical level of workers and peasants, and it also helps to promote their social and cultural integration, to level out the cultural disparities between different regions of the Ukrainian SSR and between intellectual and manual labour and to close the cultural gap between town and country. In short, the conditions required for the full and harmonious development of the personality have now been created.

In 1979, the workers of the republic and of the Soviet Union as a whole commemorated the fortieth anniversary of the reunification of all the Ukrainian lands to form a single Ukrainian Soviet state. After reunification, the western borderlands, which earlier had languished in a state of utter neglect and whose people had been condemned to a life of oppression, became a region where industry and socialist agriculture flourished and culture attained a high level, equal to that of the rest of the great Soviet family of nations.

What distinguishes cultural development in a country of advanced socialism is the growing role played by the people in cultural and artistic life, as manifested by its conscious and active involvement in creative and educational activities and in the organization of cultural pursuits. Intellectual work plays a greater part in production, the ranks of the intelligentsia swell, and it makes an increasing contribution to the building of communism. The number of specialists with a higher or secondary specialized education working in the national economy grew from 3,268,900 in 1970 to 5,087,000 on 1 January 1979; women accounted for 57.6 per cent of that number.

All this has enhanced the effectiveness of culture and has furthered its integration into all spheres of human activity, so that cultural life and everyday life interact with each other.

The unity of the people, the state and the party, together with the unity of the classes, has produced a people's state. The political, ideological and moral functions of culture, people's attitude to work and the role of education and science in the life of society—all these have been broadened and are infused with new meaning. This state of affairs is reflected in the active support given by all the people to the domestic and foreign policy of their state and government and their creative involvement in the social, political and productive life of the country. The Ukrainian people played an exceptionally active political role in the discussion centring around the draft of the new constitution of the Ukrainian SSR adopted in 1977. Some 280,000 meetings were held in factories, in people's homes and elsewhere; they were attended by over 32 million people, and 1,600,000 people took part in the actual discussion of the draft. When the entire draft of the constitution was unanimously approved, most of its articles were worded in accordance with suggestions made by the workers.

The workers were tremendously active in the elections to the Supreme Soviet of the Ukrainian SSR in 1980. Over 99.98 per cent of the voters voted for the candidates of the communist bloc and non-party members.

Of the newly-elected 650 People's Deputies, 234 are women, 204 workers, 125 collective farmers and 107 people under the age of 30. The Deputies, 488 of whom are Ukrainians, enjoy complete authority, which they exercise on behalf of the welfare of the people with the utmost competence, as befits those who are masters of their own country.

Evidence of the dynamic role played by the people can be seen in the tremendous effort they make to fulfil the plans for the development of the national economy ahead of schedule. A striking example of worker involvement is the participation of workers in the Standing Production Conferences; these conferences, which were introduced in 1958, in industrial and agricultural enterprises as a form of socialist democracy, enable workers to take part in the management and control of production. On 1 January 1979 there were over 22,000 such standing conferences, in which 1.2 million persons, including 691,500 workers, took part. At these conferences, workers compare notes about their work and make practical suggestions for improving production.

Enthusiasm for work, which is increasing steadily, is also reflected in the widespread practice of socialist emulation, the highest form of which is the movement to encourage everyone to have a conscious communist attitude towards work. Its objects are the achievement of high production indices, the continual improvement of workers' productive skills, the broadening of their cultural horizons, the development of their creative aptitudes and their active participation in social and political life. Out of the 20,000,000 persons now involved in socialist emulation, 11,500,000 are taking part in the movement for a communist attitude towards work.

The activity of the workers, together with improved production equipment and efficient organization, ensures the country's future progress. In the first four years of the current five-year plan, industrial output in the republic was one-third more than it was for the corresponding period of the previous plan. During the period 1976–80, over 2,000 new enterprises and large factories were put into operation. By 1978 industrial output in the Ukrainian SSR was 3.5 times greater than that of the whole Soviet Union in the pre-war year 1940.

Agricultural production is also on the rise. Despite adverse conditions in 1975 and 1979, the average annual volume of gross agricultural output has increased. The republic produced on an average 43,200,000 tons of grain a year, i.e. 3,200,000 tons more than during the preceding five-year plan. The production of other agricultural products and livestock is also increasing.

The national income of the Ukrainian SSR was 22 per cent greater during the tenth five-year plan than during the ninth five-year plan. Four-fifths of the national income is set aside for meeting the needs of the workers; this makes it possible to improve town planning and the provision of public services and amenities, to rebuild villages and to improve the material well-being of the people.

In accordance with the programme for social development and the improvement of the standard of living of the people, the tenth five-year plan provides for wage increases for certain categories of workers. Per capita real income in the Ukraine grew from 354 roubles in 1970 to 438 roubles in 1980; this was made possible by a significant increase in labour earnings, which outstripped rises in the costs of goods and services. Families with three dependent children received over 1,900 roubles from public funds or, as the people say, 'invisible' free state assistance. Those with more than three dependent children receive additional state benefits from public funds. The average monthly wage of workers and employees in 1980 amounted to 168.5 roubles, but, with the additional payments and advantages derived from public funds in the form of social security benefits, pensions, grants, free education and medical care, upkeep of children in pre-school institutions, sanatoria and rest-homes and other benefits, this figure was 206 roubles. The average monthly income of collective farmers increased by 30 per cent. Supplementary benefits were made available to veterans of the Great Patriotic War and families of war victims, and their housing and living conditions were improved. The pensions of workers, employees and collective farmers rose by 27.7 per cent.

Conclusion

A great deal is being done to improve the living conditions of the whole population. Ukrainians are supplied with electricity and radios. Increasing numbers of houses, hospitals, dispensaries and nursing homes are being built, and more social amenities and facilities are being provided. In the course of the last two five-year plans, 15 million people, or practically one-third of the population, have moved into new apartments or enjoy better communal housing facilities. It is worth noting that apartment rents in the republic are the lowest in the world and, on the average, do not exceed 3 per cent of a worker's family income. The people of the Ukrainian SSR have 14,400 hospitals at their disposal and health care is free. There are 34.4 doctors for every 10,000 inhabitants.

The country's achievements in the economic sphere and in science and technology, the availability of a highly skilled labour force dedicated to the ideals of communism, the enthusiastic attitude of the people towards work, the political dynamism and high cultural standard of the entire population, a climate of genuine solidarity and camaraderie, and the spirit of friendship towards all peoples, patriotism and internationalism—all these guarantee the successful implementation of the future economic strategy of the state as laid down by the Twenty-Sixth Congress of the Communist Party of the Soviet Union. Its highest goal is the steady, uninterrupted raising of the material and cultural level of the people and the creation of the conditions most conducive to the harmonious development of the personality.

If this noble goal is to be attained, peace is necessary. The Ukrainian people, together with all the peoples of the USSR, are wholeheartedly committed to the cause of peace and are firmly convinced that peace will inevitably triumph.

Titles in this series:

The serial numbering of titles in this series, the presentation of which has been modified, was discontinued with the volume *Cultural policy in Italy*